SPARE RIBS
Women in the Humor Biz

SPARE RIBS
Women in the Humor Biz

DENISE COLLIER
KATHLEEN BECKETT
With Photographs by Nancy Rica Schiff

ST. MARTIN'S PRESS, NEW YORK

Library of Congress Cataloging in Publication Data

Collier, Denise.
Spare ribs.
1.   Women television personalities—United States—
Biography. 2. Women comedians—United States—
Biography. I. Beckett, Kathleen, joint author.
II. Title.
PN1992.8.W65C6   791.45'092'2 [B]   79-27523
ISBN 0-312-75011-0

Acknowledgments
I would also like to thank the following folks who provided support and inspiration, soft drugs and hard cash when the chips were down: Lee Marrs, for getting the ball rolling; Terri Tobin; Gail "Mama" Gottlieb; Michael "no egg creams" Palin; Patrick Stansfield; Weavie; Elliott Randall; Genevieve Roudiez; Pauline Neuwirth; Ma and Pa Collier; Duke; Bull; Hans Fantel; Bonni Kogen; Angela Bucalo; Kevin Quinn Avery; J.D.; and Nancy Nancy Nancy.

–D.C.

For Sasha, with love
—D.C.

For my Mother and Father
—K.B.

Table of Contents

Introduction

Humor is one of the hottest topics around today. It's no longer considered just light matinée entertainment, but a big box office draw, capable of turning repertory company players into media superstars. The top-rated shows on television are all situation comedies—in fact, some of the brightest new talent seen on TV today was discovered in comedy cabarets such as New York's Improvisation, Los Angeles' Comedy Store and Chicago's Second City. More and more, comedy is being recognized as a vital, progressive art form that reflects our aspirations and our anxieties.

As is happening in every field, humor is at last opening up for women. They are going for the laughs and recognition in all aspects; writing, cartooning, producing, performing on television, in movies and on the stage. Women are proving that they can be bright, assertive, attractive and funny—that they have a sense of humor and are no longer timid about expressing it.

Comedy is a business that has traditionally been the domain of males, and their influence still dominates—in numbers, in attitude, and in determining the way things are done and who does them. Women have, in some cases, had difficulty making "female-related" material understood by men. Some women, especially those who perform, run into an image problem—the difficulty of retaining their femininity while being funny. Attractiveness combined with the ability to make others laugh seems to be too much of a good thing: Both bring with them attention and power.

In its extreme, humor can exert a devastating put-down power when others are the brunt of a joke. Even in its milder forms, it can smack of assertiveness, intelligence, independence. For some of the women we interviewed, humor is a political tool, used to even the odds in a male-dominated world. For others, it is simply a natural way of dealing with the absurdities of life, an expression of inner exuberance. Each of these women, in her personal and professional life, has used humor to get what she wanted—to cajole a strict parent, to apologize to school-mates for being too smart, to laugh at faults or weaknesses before others could, to land a job, to persuade others of her point of view, to help get over the rough spots in a relationship—to help get through life.

We had originally intended to profile five women humorists for a magazine article, but each time we interviewed someone, she would suggest one or two other women who were doing something new in humor. We followed their leads and finally chose the seventeen women we interviewed in depth. We include profiles of women who are solid successes, some who are up and coming, others who are still struggling to be recognized.

We wanted to find out certain things from these women: why they chose humor as a career and how they got started in it; pitfalls they encountered and lessons they learned along the way; who influenced them and in what ways; how growing up female shaped their style and choice of material; how they feel about becoming models for others; where they see comedy heading; what's funny to them and how they make it come across effectively to others.

For a sense of perspective, we spoke with two all-time great comediennes, Phyllis Diller and Joan Rivers. We have included their reflections on what it was like to be female pioneers in the virtually all-male field of stand-up comedy.

By using the interview format, we gained a sense of intimacy with each of these women. The work on this book has turned out to be a collaboration not only of two authors and a photographer, but all who were involved. We found a great spirit of cooperation and trust—and a lot of laughs.

SPARE RIBS
Women in the Humor Biz

The way it was

OF ALL the avenues in humor women can pursue, stand-up comedy has got to be the toughest. The proving grounds are dingy clubs, often filled with audiences of persistent hecklers. The hours are long and late and require anxiously awaiting the nod to go on, which usually comes after the busboy has been given his chance. The pay is low or nonexistent, and the peer group of other women to turn to for support is minuscule. A look around at the number of women who have made successful careers in stand-up comedy confirms the grim prospects.

Tremendous mettle is required for a woman to stand alone on a stage and attempt to capture the attention and amuse an assortment of skeptics who have paid hard cash for a good time. Most women don't consider the possibility. Many become discouraged and give up. A few make it.

Phyllis Diller and Joan Rivers broke the sexual barrier in the field of stand-up comedy more than a decade ago. They are also credited with originating a style of humor strongly based on one-liners about husbands, housework and unhappiness with their appearance—a style traditionally labeled "self-deprecatory." We spoke to Diller and Rivers to find out why they do it and how they became so successful at it.

Phyllis Diller

ALTHOUGH I did not think that the real Phyllis Diller would be exactly like her stage persona—the loopy lady in the sequined tent dress, ankle-high go-go boots and platinum hair that looks like one of Dolly Parton's wigs gone through the wash—I was not prepared for the beautiful woman dressed in heather-colored suede who greeted me in the drawing room of her Beverly Hills mansion.

Phyllis Diller has been in show business for twenty-five years. She is as much a part of my comedy consciousness as Lucille Ball or Ernie Kovacs. I was curious to find out just what motivates a woman to get up on a stage, alone, in front of hundreds of people and try to fill the time with laughter. What Phyllis told me is a genuinely moving account of her brave dream to fulfill her own potential and make good the promise of a better life for her five children. She is a warm, vivacious, witty woman who knows exactly where she came from, where she's heading and who she is today.

–D.C.

Becoming a comedienne was my way of adjusting to puberty. When I reached that self-conscious age where I looked like Olive Oyl and wanted to look like Jean Harlow, I knew something had to be done. From twelve on, the only way to handle the terror of social situations was comedy—break the ice, make everybody laugh. I did it to make people feel more relaxed, including myself.

I started doing comedy professionally in clubs in 1955. That's twenty-five years ago! I can scarcely believe it. But I didn't start this career on my own. I didn't even know I was funny. My husband insisted that I try to do comedy and for two years we argued about it. I said, "You're out of your mind! Haven't you noticed that we have children—these five little rug-rats are ours?" He simply nagged and nagged and so one day I said okay. From then on I started thinking—how do you become a comedienne? Well, first you gotta get a job, so I picked up the phone and called the Red Cross and said, "I'm available for shows. Where do you want me?" They immediately sent me to the Presidio in San Francisco and I went from ward to ward and did shows with my son. He played the banjo and I played the piano. We did some music, told some jokes, tried to be funny. Mostly the patients just stared at us, but they were glad to have anyone there.

I was the *first* stand-up comedienne. There was no Totie [Fields] and no Joan [Rivers] when I started out. My first response to going professional was rejection. At first, nothing seemed to work. I was a normal-looking woman—dark brown hair, wearing perfectly normal clothes that I bought off the racks—and I'd come out and try to be funny. The audience thought I was the lady down the street, which is exactly what I was. A guy whose club I worked in and who knew a bit about comedy said, "You smile too much. Be hostile." I had spent all my life trying to throw out hostility from my personal life, to be a nice, open channel for good, you see. I couldn't understand what he meant. Now I'm doing it. I got a review the other day that said "bitchy," which is what you gotta do. Back then I was sweet. I was too sweet. My voice was sweet. Now I have developed what it is you have to have to be a successful comic.

People back then were not ready for a lady comic. They

had no basis for acceptance. "It's a *woman!* What's she trying to do?" "She's got to be an ugly person." "She's got to be a butch person." "She's got to be a nasty woman." Not true at all. No one is more feminine than I. I'm basically a mother and a wife and a grandmother and all those good things. But to make it on stage, I had to make fun of myself first. I had to dress funny, I had to cover my figure—and I have an excellent figure—or I couldn't make any body jokes. Of course, I was accused of being self-deprecatory. I've got to be. Look, Don Rickles is other-people-deprecatory. Comedy is tragedy revisited or hostility. It is mock hostility, of course, or it would be ugly; we would have a war. But I would come out on stage and put everybody down—myself, the children, the lady next door, the cops. Everybody has got to be bad. See, if everything is good, you've got Grace Kelly and that's not funny. I have fat jokes, skinny jokes, drunk jokes, idiot jokes—they're categories, they're not actual people I'm poking fun at. There's no reality whatsoever in my act. It's all for fun.

Naturally, I talked about things I knew. Nobody was doing any kid jokes because they were all male comics. They did their mother-in-law jokes and wife jokes. So I did husband jokes. You know, that's a whole field that's untapped, untouched. I was the first to go after the husbands. It was always my wife, the idiot. Now it's my husband, the idiot. Right on. My goal at the very beginning was to get everyone from one to one hundred to like my work. Today that's whom I have. My first group of supporters were homosexuals, the second group and my most avid fans were women. I was saying things about kids, husbands, mothers-in-law, things that they wanted to say but couldn't. Then the men realized that I was a normal human being and they became fans. Old people like me; even children like me. I'm a sure thing. I'm a hit. Presold. They laugh and scratch when I come out on stage, greet me as if I were an old friend, which I am.

There are probably one thousand homosexuals who regularly impersonate me at parties or in small clubs. And there are women who dress up and go to parties as me. If you produce a strong character, which I do, you are easy to imitate. People do Bette Davis, they do Tallulah, they do Katharine Hepburn. They use someone who has a certain style.

I'm a comic, not a comic actress, and there's a big difference. A comic works in "one," alone. A comic actress works "ensembles." I do a character known as Phyllis Diller, but the stage character, of course, has nothing to do with the real person.

On stage I am abrasive, strong. Everybody thinks I'm a large woman, they think I'm tall. The first thing they say when they meet me offstage is, "God, you're so *small!*" The next thing they say is, "My God, you're so pretty, you're so feminine!" You see, what I do on stage has nothing to do with reality. That is a character I'm playing. I play classical piano seriously and when I do my symphony act, it's a totally different character. I am Grande Dame Illya Dillya in a long gown and tiara with egret feathers. Oh, she's so grand!

I was very secure as a child. I was an only child. I had all the attention, all the love, I got all the money when my folks died. My parents were teetotalers. They paid cash for cars. They weren't wealthy, but they were well organized and very bright. But at first that childhood security didn't carry over into my professional life. I had learned it but I didn't understand it until I got hold of a book called *The Magic of Believing*, and then everything I had been taught and fed. . . . Well, it's all in the Bible, but it's such funny wording. It's in all the great philosophies, this thread of truth that flows through everything. "All things work together for those who love." I would attribute a lot of my success to that book. You see, I had the talent, I knew that. I know what I'm capable of and to not do it, to not be able to do it is a drag. You see, I had given up everything to become a stand-up comedienne. I gave up my house, my kids went to live with relatives and I went on the road with no home. I realized that I was married to a man who was never going to be able to make a living. I had all those kids because I wanted them. But the marriage was not good, and in those days divorce was practically out of the question. I waited until I had gone through all of my inheritance, and then I went to work. My jobs kept leading to better and better ones. There is no motivation like a mother with her young. Nothing was going to stop me. I had to get them an education and a home. But my kids were never bereft. I made them a promise that they would have a beautiful home and a pool and a horse if they wanted one. And now they've traveled all over the world and they have had everything. Just look around this house—I didn't let them down, did I?

Joan Rivers

I MET Joan Rivers at a Long Island music theater, where she was appearing with singer Bobby Vinton. The program for the show listed Joan's impressive credits: "comedienne in residence" at the MGM Grand Hotel in Las Vegas, more than three hundred appearances on "The Tonight Show," author of a book (*Having a Baby Can Be a Scream*), a Broadway show (*Fun City*), a television movie (*The Girl Most Likely To*), plus numerous screenplays, including *Rabbit Test*, which she also directed.

I saw Joan's act first—she pranced energetically from one end of the stage to the other, dressed all in black save for a long, printed scarf that trailed behind her. She delivered a forty-five-minute monologue without a

pause—except for laughter. Backstage in her dressing
room after the show, she also spoke without a pause,
offering opinions and answers without hesitation, effort-
lessly weaving in humorous asides.

—K.B.

There are so few women stand-up comediennes for two
reasons. One is that it's a very lonely life on the road and I
think a lot of girls, after doing it for a little while, realize
how horrendous it is. You stop because it's just too awful.
The reason that I survive is that I write, so I have a double
thing going. I'm never lonely, because I go home to
something. But to spend two weeks in Milwaukee without knowing anyone. . . . If you're a man you can go into
a bar, so it's much easier. For a woman, you just cannot
go out after you're up and happy. You go back to your
hotel room and hope they have late night movies. The
second reason is television. Everybody, lately, who starts
out as a stand-up in The Comedy Store, which is where
they're all coming from now, or The Improvisation, is
immediately picked up for a series, so they're being
pulled away from the stable quickly.

Women now have much more access than before. The
only sad thing about lady stand-up comics now is they
think they have to do "women's humor." There is no
women's humor. I have fights all the time about this. If
something is funny, it's funny. Dorothy Parker would be
considered funny whether she was a man or a woman;
Clare Boothe Luce was hysterical.

Also, you change a lot according to your audience. If
the audience is married, settled, blue-collar, you're not
going to do Proust jokes, you're not going to get into
wonderful references from Aristotle. You try to deal with
housewife things. I'm a woman, I know I'm a woman, so
the humor that comes out of me is going to be from my
point of view.

I think I lead the audience, the men in the audience, well enough into it that they can understand it. It's all fundamental, what I talk about—women's problems. You just bring them in slowly and create a visual picture.

The only time I have terrible trouble dealing with people is in front of a totally male audience. Every once in a while they'll call me up and say, "GM is having a luncheon, can you fly to Detroit and do something?" In the past I would have gone, but now I will not if there are no women in the audience.

You need women to relate to because the men relate to you through the women they are with, and then they go forward. But when I've had an all-male audience, I've bombed. I haven't done it in five years. It's just that my topics, because they're me, are automatically about my child, whom they really couldn't care about, and housework. But nowadays, you're not allowed to talk about that, because women say that's not what we're all about. But the original mother-in-law joke is from a Greek play, in which they say to the man, "How is your mother-in-law?" and he says, "Immortal." That made me laugh because there are mother-in-law jokes going back to ancient Greece. Nothing changes—but girls are having trouble thinking what women's topics are.

Sex is a good topic for everybody. Comedy is changing radically, thank goodness. We're all here because of Lenny Bruce—he broke the barrier. That means for the men as well as the women. Bruce said, "This is what I'm talking about and it's really true." So, obviously, sex comes out of that. But it has nothing to do with women and men. I talk about sex in my act about as far as I would talk about it in private with my friends. I don't know what the barriers are because I just pretend I'm in a living room. I guess you could talk more freely in the living room than you did ten years ago, but I'm not aware of it.

I used to see Lenny Bruce every night in Greenwich

Village, right during his whole end period, when I was starting out. Jack Benny, whose poise we still do not have, I admire too. And Lucille Ball because I think she's a brilliant sketch comedienne; she's the best in the world. If you watch her time, you can clock it.

I never found doors shut in the clubs because I was in the Village at the right time, whatever that time was. I was at the right time for the bright new girl to come on Johnny Carson and be irreverent. But I've had nothing but doors slammed in my face in the movies. I've never come across so many closed doors, so many people thinking I was incapable, that a woman could not deal with it, a woman could not handle a crew, a woman could not in any way, shape or form be able to control a movie set or know what is funny.

I think of myself as a writer. I became a stand-up because it was a way to make a living. It sounds so stupid. I was originally an actress and nobody cared, and a writer and nobody cared, so friends of mine said, "Go to the Village, you can pass the hat, you can make money," and that's how I started being a comic. I'd pass the hat and get six or seven dollars. Great!

Young women who want to get started in stand-up should do it, that's the main thing. Stop talking about it. Work anywhere. If your audience isn't bright, take this as a challenge, an intellectual challenge of, "Can I reach them?" Some audiences, when they're bright, could come into your home and I always like to feel those are the ones I'm dealing with, those that would be my friends. And some audiences you look at and say, "Can I relate to this lady who's got curlers in her hair and a kerchief?" and that makes me very proud that they like me at the end. So work to anybody, take any job in the world, sneak in anywhere you can and write, write, write, because if you write your own, that's the whole thing.

If people think I make fun of my appearance, it's

because (I'll be very honest) if I thought I was terrific looking I wouldn't be doing it. I think you should say what you think, and be what you think, onstage. So I do it for that reason and also, I think it relaxes your audience tremendously. If you come on with a superior attitude, they cannot relate to you. And you must relate in comedy, you must be friends or you have no chance at all. I let them know at the very start that I don't think I'm so special.

Whether you're a man or a woman, when you get up there onstage the audience is already looking up, visually, so you have to relax them. You can't be smarter than they are. If you're going to mention something in the news, you must let them assume they read it too. I'll say, "You saw in the paper. . . ." and then I'll tell them exactly what they didn't see, that they assume they saw. I do a tremendous amount of that because nobody, when they're paying money, should be embarrassed or made to feel inferior.

I think as you get older you're much more conservative. I don't know if we all become our parents—I hope not— but I always say that you get married, you get the mortgage and suddenly you realize this is it. God! And the humor changes too. Older people are not as open to new ideas. College audiences will laugh at anything. They're totally irreverent. It's your brightest time and it's wonderful because they know what you mean.

I'm totally schizophrenic. The older ladies think I'm going to do housework jokes so I always throw them in. They pay, they deserve six housework jokes. Las Vegas is an older crowd—you never see young people in Vegas. Could be economics, and also, I don't think a young bright crowd says, "Hey, let's hit Vegas for the weekend and catch Sammy and Sinatra and Petula and Mitzy and Joan!"

Everyone forgets I was the first lady ever to come on

television and laugh about being single, laugh about all that nonsense and also the first lady to bring Betty Friedan on television, on "The Mike Douglas Show," and deal with those issues. I always tell feminists that my life is a feminist life—just turn around, you idiots. I have done a movie—I cast it, got my own money, did my own editing—what do you want from me?

I studied with Margaret Mead at Columbia University when I was an anthropology major at Barnard College. When I realized, unfortunately, that I was going to have to go through the nightclub route, I called up Margaret Mead, just at the start of the women's liberation movement, back in 1966. I said, "You know, I'm all over the country and we could do surveys and find out what women think." What people in New York think is not interesting because we all think "Bloomingdale's." But what do women think in Montana, Michigan, Wyoming? She wrote a survey for me and I used to go into nightclubs—when you think of the nerve!—and place them at every table, right next to the minimum cards, four little pencils and mimeographed sheets. We did this survey, and bundles were going back to Columbia from all over the country. It was fascinating to see the change in women's attitudes. We had questions like, "Who should rule the house?" And the answer was always, "My husband a little bit more than me." "Do you think women should work?"—"No." Look how far we've come.

Zora Rasmussen

VOGUE calls her "a tall, cuddly, blonde armful of a look-at-me girl." The *Village Voice* calls her "a gum-popping frizzy blonde." Me, I'd call her crazy, in the absolutely best sense of the word. Ask her a question and she's good for a half hour, describing what it's like to drive a Good Humor truck, to waitress, to perform *Hair* in Africa—and somewhere in the middle, answering the question with insight and intelligence.

Zora amassed a cult of followers in New York City, fans who returned repeatedly every Saturday night to the nightclub, Reno Sweeney, to enjoy her "Late Nite Madness." Zora would clown, sing and delight—until the show had to close when the management was no longer allowed to book acts with back-up bands. Just another setback that somehow, with perseverance and pluck, Zora always manages to turn into a springboard for something even better.

–K.B.

I was funny when I was a kid because I was ugly. I wasn't ugly, but I wasn't cute—I was a cootie. Want to see

13

my picture? I use this in my act. I ask everybody, "If you were popular in high school, will you please raise your hands?" No one does. Then I say, "Sometimes when you think about the past you're a little hard on yourself. I just want you to be the judge—was I that bad?" See.

Oh my God.

Who invented these glasses? I look like the back of a Plymouth.

How old were you then?

Twelve going on fifty-one.

Kids can be so cruel at that age. How did you survive school?

I wanted to get back at everybody and be a concert pianist. I'd see myself playing a concert piano and everyone would applaud. When I got into junior high, I was weird. I was funny, but kids think if you're funny, then you're weird. But the first approval I got was in junior high when I did a pantomime. I mouthed, "Just You Wait, Henry Higgins" and Michael Hewitt came up to me and said, "That was really good" so I thought, "If Michael Hewitt thinks I'm good, I'll go into the theater."

Was Michael Hewitt the Big Man on Campus?

He was a minuscule guy who was one of the popular guys at school. He was a cool kid and I wasn't cool. I had a lousy self-image.

If you take away the glasses, though, that's a pretty face. But I guess at that age kids don't see through the glasses.

People don't pick up on the face, they pick up on how you think of yourself. I thought terribly of myself. But this pantomime number gave me some confidence, so in high school I was in plays. I'd always get character roles—I'd play older women. Then one day I saw the Coty Combo, a stage band—they had songs like "Girl Talk"—all those terrible, chauvinistic songs. And I saw them singing and said, "I want that," to sing with the Coty Combo. So I did, with the glasses and wearing a formal gown. I thought I was Barbra Streisand. I sang "Pe-e-eople," things like that.

I wanted to be in the theater, I always did. I used to tell Hazel at my father's factory, "I want to live in New York," and she'd say, "Ha ha ha." She'd laugh. "Yes, I am, I'm going to live in New York, I'm going to be an actress. I'm going to have an apartment for $500 a month." Well, I am an actress, I live in New York. My apartment, however, is $185. For $185 you can't beat it, except for the guy downstairs who uses his apartment for a kitty litter box. It smells; it's terrible.

Before New York, I went to college, and that's when hippies happened. I'm of the generation that got stoned before they got drunk. So I became this hippie, but I wasn't really good as a hippie because the role structures were just the same. The girls made the brownies, the guys got high. So I just didn't fit in as a hippie and I wanted to be a singer in show business, but at that time, everyone was, like, "Oh wow, it's Janis Joplin!" I thought, "How am I gonna sing?" I sing a different way. More like Dionne Warwick. I was driving an ice cream truck at the time for Good Humor, selling to all these kids who were sugar junkies. Kids would be mainlining rocket pops—they really had a habit. So while I was doing that, there were auditions for *Hair* and I thought, "Oh, wow, I want to be in *Hair!*" So I auditioned and I sang a Laura Nyro song and there were twelve thousand girls trying out and I was singing and it got down to two hundred and I was still singing and it got down to fifty, to twenty, to eleven—and I was still singing! They needed eight. I didn't get it. What a bummer.

Let me tell you, it hasn't been easy for me. For some people, it's like, "You want a TV series?—here" But not for me. But when I didn't get a part in *Hair* I kept calling the show—I had balls, you know—and asked if they needed a replacement. I kept calling up and I finally got it. I was one of only three people who got to go on the national tour. So it's always bad turns and me not giving up that makes it a good turn.

So I went in *Hair* and saved a lot of money and moved to New York. I moved in with a guy, Robert I., while I was finding a place to stay. But I married him. We're separated now, but we're still very close. He's an actor and he wrote a show called *The Dementos*. It's crazy, about bag people. I play a punk rocker named Spike Heal—Spike because she's a reincarnation of Spike Jones and Heal because she's healed by God. Then I did "High Heeled Women," but it was called "Funny Ladies" at the time—the first comedy act with all women. I did it in 1977 and comedy was just starting to happen then as it is now. It's a big thing now, especially women in comedy.

What made you think of doing a comedy act with all women?

Because it was such a pain for me to go to places like The Improv and Catch a Rising Star and wait so long to go on. I'd have to go on at three in the morning—at that time the audience is like Dawn of the Dead. So I thought, "I don't want to do that. I'm going to create a showcase. But what can be different about the showcase?" Then I thought, "All women. There's nothing with all women." So I went to a club owner and told him I have a great idea, and not only is it a good idea, but it's also good copy, because nothing has been written about women comedians. I put an ad in *Show Business* and got all these girls and auditioned them. We had the group and they all did ten minutes and I was able to do twenty. It was like I had a place where I could show my act.

What is it about stand-up that makes it so hard for women? It's hard for anybody, but there are so few women.

I think there are so few women because it's just

happening for women now, so it takes a while to get it going. But there are a lot more women now than there were when I started in '77.

Why weren't as many women trying it then?

Maybe because there wasn't all the publicity about it, so it wasn't thought of as an alternative. Here in New York there are still very few. And I sing as well as do comedy—I'm bi.

When you first started doing stand-up, how did audiences react? Were they receptive? Surprised?

I think at first it's better if you're a woman because the audience is curious. You get more attention, you have more of a chance. I don't think it's particularly harder for women, and now showcase clubs like The Improv want women.

I was talking to the manager there who said he'd love women to come and try out, but not many do. I did see there, recently, a woman who did a lot of jokes about sex, which were greeted with dead silence.

Well, I'm revamping my act now and I'm thinking of putting something in it about sex. I want to talk about my own experiences, like how the first time I had sex I felt like Peggy Lee—is that all there is? The approach I would have is a woman's approach—how women feel about sex. I'm not doing pussy jokes, and I'm not saying, "And he was hung like this!" That's so disgusting. You see, in comedy, I don't want to hear about commercials, I don't want to hear about the subway, I don't want to hear bathroom humor. Richard Pryor uses sex, but it's done with sensitivity and there's a point to it. I think it would be interesting for a woman who's vulnerable to talk about her viewpoint on sex. But some comediennes are very tough about it. I don't think women have to play the victim all the time when they talk about "the guys trying to pick me up." There's a lot more to sex than looking at it negatively. You can talk about sex and make it funny but you don't have to castrate men. I don't think it's men against women in comedy, really. I think, in fact, it might be harder for a man going into comedy now because there have been so many men in comedy that all the styles are tapped. For women, it's like the great frontier, you have more of a chance.

Have you ever felt that women in the audience understood what you were talking about, but not the men?

No, because what I do is talk about my personal experiences—from the viewpoint of a woman, yes, but I don't "ghettoize" my language just to relate to women. I think it's important, if you're an entertainer, that you relate to everybody. I want to relate to people in suits and ties and people who wear beads in their noses. Comedy is a form of relating the way you feel about things. I talk about high school. Girls will laugh at this picture, but guys feel the same way. Everyone felt a little inadequate when he or she was in high school. It's not like I'm putting myself down. What I'm saying is essentially, "Look how we were then and how we thought and look how we are now. Aren't we much better off?" It's like that Robert Frost poem, "The Road Not Taken." There's a road that everyone's taken that's easier and there's the other one not taken that's harder. I think for a lot of people who went through a childhood like this, it forces you to take the road that's not taken, the harder one, but eventually it's much more fulfilling. I go into a sad song after I show the picture. I like that transition, bringing the audience through ebbs and tides, ups and downs.

Is that a powerful feeling, to be able to move an audience like that?

Not only that, it's fun because the audience is able to experience a lot of emotions. Singing is more introspective. You can be thinking about the dishes at home. But comedy is more assaultive, it demands attention. Someone is speaking. So I mix the two mediums. At first some people said I should just do comedy or just sing. But I've always stuck to my guns and said, "No, I won't. I'll do both." I like to do both because I think I do both well.

Vogue and *The Village Voice* seem to seize upon the fact that not only are you a comedienne and a singer, but you're great looking as well.

Humor to me is sexy. If I like a man, it's very important that he make me laugh. It's like verbal intercourse. So instead of playing down the way I look, when I go on stage I want to get dressed up as much as possible. I think that when you're onstage, people want to look at something that looks good. You look at Steve Martin—he has a total look, right? Woody Allen has a look. Robin Williams has a look. I think it's important for women in comedy at this point to have a look. Phyllis Diller had a look—it wasn't glamorous, but it was a look. So this is the type of thing I'm going after, to have a definite sort of image. And I want to be glamorous, like the 1940s. Betty Hutton was real cute. But she wasn't stand-up, either. So I'm trying to mix all elements together. Singing melancholy as well as funny songs, doing stand-up and then doing monologues of a character. I want to work on a "That Girl" character—everything's so wonderful. But I want to relate it to me and I want to have the optimism of "That Girl" while everything is falling apart around me. Because that's how it is with me. I try to get that optimism when everything's always falling apart. So I'm going to work on that character.

How do you work on characters?

I work with a friend, Scott Whitman. And it comes through development. I just started to work on character comedy—it's a fairly new area for me and I want to start tapping it.

What about your other material?

It comes from my experiences, and then a lot of it is changed through my insight. Recently Richard Pryor has influenced me a lot. He uses physicality to accentuate a punch line. He'll say something and then he'll act it out and that makes it funny.

Is that something you've used?

I have because I'm a physical comedienne, but I want to work on it more.

What do you mean by "physical comedienne"?

I make faces and move my arms and carry on. Some people say that it's self-deprecating—why make faces? That's what comedy is. Chevy Chase falls down—they don't say it's self-deprecating. George Carlin will pick his nose. That's not self-deprecating. That's *funny*. Women should have the same license. I'll do anything—I don't stop and think of whether it's feminine or not. I just think of me. I think the distinction between being a lady or not is breaking down. Now we are just being ourselves. That's what I'm trying to do—be myself. I hope that people like me, and I just want more people to like me. I'm not trying to teach people anything about women, or teach them *my* viewpoint. It's just the world according to me. This is how I see my world, and so I share that. I let the audience experience the way I think. And then, hopefully, they laugh sometimes. I just want them to laugh, that's all. Make 'em laugh!

Anne Beatts

WHEN I met Anne, she was in her office at Rockefeller Center writing a skit for "NBC's Saturday Night Live," propped up in the hospital bed she substitutes for the more conventional desk and chair arrangement (the food tray holds her typewriter) and wearing an antique silk kimono and pointed sunglasses from the 1950s.

On the strength of two Emmy Awards for her work at "Saturday Night Live," her former editorship at the *National Lampoon,* and her coeditorship of *Titters: The First Book of Humor by Women,* Anne could be considered one of the most successful writers of comedy today. She's in her early thirties, has a direct manner of speaking that's frequently punctuated with a giggling laugh and has strong views on the subjects of humor and women.

–K.B.

Have you had any problems being a woman humorist?

Sure. Vocabulary, for instance, is a major problem. At "Saturday Night Live" I collaborate with another woman writer and when people ask us, "Why do you collaborate?'' we always say, ''Self-defense.'' It's frustrating to find that your humor can be unintelligible to others. Together, since we both understand each other, we are now able to make our point of view intelligible to men. But first of all, we each had to find someone else who shared the same vocabulary and reference points.

Last night, for example, we were working on a sketch and came up with a line that we thought was wonderful: ''Tell Granny Loopner only twenty-eight more cloves and her pomander ball will be finished.'' We tried this line out on one of the male writers and he just shrugged his shoulders. We said, ''Do you know what a pomander ball is?'' ''No.'' So then we said, ''Do you know what cloves are?'' and he said, ''Do you mean garlic cloves?'' So we went around and asked three different men, ''What are cloves?'' and none of them knew. Finally, we asked Lorne Michaels, the producer, and he said, ''Well, it's a spice, right?'' I guess that's why he's the producer.

I can still remember feeling a little indentation in my thumb from pressing those goddamn cloves into the orange. And you finally get one in and the clove part falls off and you have to use another one. It's a big production. But I'm faced with the question of, ''Can we put that line over? Will there be enough women in the room who will know?'' There's a reluctance to use it.

What did you end up doing with the line?
We didn't use it.

Has it ever happened that the men writers have felt the need to ask the women, ''Do you understand this?''
No. They never say, ''Do you know what a carburetor is?'' Never. Okay, pomander ball I could understand their not knowing. But cloves? Haven't they ever eaten baked ham? They've never noticed, they've never baked a ham, they've never hung around the kitchen on Easter while mother put cloves in the ham. There is a women's culture that men just don't know about. So when they say ''Hey,

that joke's not funny," it's sometimes because they don't understand the vocabulary. They don't understand what the joke is based on.

You hear people talk about women's humor as a form of ghetto humor, but unlike other people who have ghetto humor, we don't have a ghetto. We're separated, we're all in our own little kitchens. The ghetto humorists of the '60s—Godfrey Cambridge, Dick Gregory—supposedly told the jokes that black people laugh at when there aren't any white people around. Well, they had a chance to be together without any white people around. I'm not saying that was enviable, but they did. But women don't have much of a chance to be in groups together without any men around. They are isolated, they are in nuclear families, they're all in their little households. Women don't really get much of a chance to spend time together after they get out of school, unless they happen to work in a job where there are a lot of other women. But if they take the traditional step—get married and have kids—then maybe they get to go out with the girls one night a week and they talk about the kids. They don't develop their humor any further.

Also, when women are funny they're often called bitchy or catty. So you are reluctant to be too witty, because if you make a witty remark about somebody, other people might think you're being a cat. Women aren't encouraged to be funny. They don't have much of a chance to be in a free situation exchanging thoughts with other women. They're too isolated and they're too wrapped up with their own lives. That's what I mean when I say we don't have a ghetto. Maybe we should start one. Just rent a building and put a big banner outside saying WOMEN'S GHETTO. The lack of that is one of the reasons it has taken so long for women's humor to break through.

Sometimes I'll have conversations with women who

went to women's colleges and they'll say, "We were all funny, we used to laugh all the time." And I'll say, "But were there any men in the room?" That's the question that's got to be asked. And they will think about it and realize that once they get out of that segregated atmosphere and into the world of men, the women who were terrific cut-ups in all-girls' high schools and women's colleges will stop being funny. Because they have to. They're afraid to.

Why?

I think they're afraid to take the spotlight away from the men. They're afraid to speak out because they're afraid that their jokes will not be appreciated by men. They might revolve around the word "clove" and men won't know it and they won't laugh. I can remember articles in *Seventeen* when I was growing up that said, "Discuss his interests, ask him what he likes. If he's interested in cars, learn about cars and talk to him about cars."

Read the sports page.

I still do that. If I got out with a new man, I think "Oh, what is he interested in?" And I say, "Oh, basketball? Oh really?"

Do you think that's just human? If you were meeting a new woman friend, wouldn't you want to know what she was interested in?

I don't think that there were articles in *Playboy* or *Rogue* or the magazines boys read in high school that told them to ask girls about needlepoint. You heard a lot back then about the "child-centered home." Well, I think it was the *boy*-centered home. The attitude from the mother and all the women the boy ran into when he was starting to date was that he was the pearl in their oyster and that they were supposed to pay attention to what he thought and what he wanted to do. It would even say in *Seventeen*— "Let *him* choose the restaurant."

So the woman is just a foil. Being funny is too much of an assertion, too much evidence that there's a brain operating.

It's too aggressive, because it's saying, "Hey, look at me! I'm funny!" And you were never encouraged to do that. A nice girl did not draw attention to herself. A girl could draw attention to herself by being beautiful but even then you were not supposed to dress in a way that was overtly erotic. That was wrong too, that was considered trampy. You were allowed to be "pert 'n' perky" but that was about it. Our magazines would say, "Laugh at his jokes." Well I don't think that the "Playboy Adviser" even *now* says, "Laugh at *her* jokes."

How did you handle this when you were that age?

I would be a pal. I went through a phase of being a guy's pal, of being "just like a boy." "Gee," they would say, "she's almost like one of us!"

She doesn't even know what a clove is.

Right. That was always my role at the *National Lampoon* —"not bad for a girl." I have a theory about American men—I think they think women are boys who don't know how to throw a ball very well. American women are forced into the role of being men without penises, of being men who haven't quite been able to make it. If women don't want to be pussycats, then they get forced into the role of being almost as good as men. Which is lousy. And it took me until recently to realize that it was a pretty poor deal, and that was partly as a result of my experience at the *National Lampoon*, where I was one of the guys, except I wasn't one of the guys and I could never be anything better than a second-rate guy. So you lose.

You lose especially in the field of humor. And some women put themselves in that position. If women are with men, say on a date, they will watch to see whether the men are laughing at a joke before they will laugh. Whereas if they were in a room full of women they would laugh spontaneously. But I can see the women in our audience taking their cues from their escorts. I've tried jokes on mixed and segregated audiences and I'll find that there will be, in the mixed, a laugh from the men, a pause and then a back-laugh from the women. It sounds weird but it's true.

What sort of things went over well with the women alone that didn't in a mixed audience?

Any material that might be sexual or risqué. In one of the lectures I give to college groups I say that I've discovered that men hate women and why they do. They hate them because women can always have sex—even when they're dead. Men have to be in the mood but women can always do it. They can be asleep or they can be dead; it doesn't matter. Women will laugh at that at women's schools, but in coed schools, they will hesitate to see whether the men can swallow it and then they will laugh—but not immediately.

Do you think, in this instance, the women are afraid that the men will think they are laughing at them and not being the adoring, supportive female that *Seventeen* said they should be?

Right. I think that the reason men are so hung up and so afraid of women being funny—especially attractive women, they don't mind if fat, old, ugly women are funny—is because they link it with sexuality and they unconsciously are afraid that the ultimate joke will be the size of their sexual apparatus. There's a little trigger in a man's mind when he hears a woman laughing that makes him think, "She's laughing at me because I'm not big enough."

And that's why someone like Joan Rivers is not a threat because you know she's going to be laughing at the lack of size in her own sexual apparatus?

Yes. She's continually putting herself down and so the

men are safe. In fact, she isn't unattractive, but she's taken herself further in that direction, and I think for this reason. Phyllis Diller too—she's like a caricature. And Mae West was funny and sexual but she too was a caricature, like a cartoon, because she was beyond sex. Marilyn Monroe was slightly cartoon-like in her comedy. She used to play the dumb blonde who accidentally said some penetrating and witty things, but it was always an accident that the words came out of her mouth. So that removed the threat.

You have to go back to the '30s and '40s before you can find any woman who was attractive, intelligent and funny. Carole Lombard, Katharine Hepburn, the early Rosalind Russell. They could all make jokes. If you look at "The Thin Man" comedies, Myrna Loy (even though she played the good wife) still gets drunk, she flirts, she's funny and witty and she often tops her husband.

Why weren't they seen as threats?

I think that what happened socially was that women became more liberated after getting the vote, so the '30s was a liberated period of women and the image of women. Women were allowed to express themselves, both their sexuality and their humor, at the same time. You'll see heroines of the '30s actually decide to keep their jobs and remain independent. That's the kind of comedy we should be doing now. You see women holding their own, not just as dippy blondes but as intelligent women who work and wisecrack at the same time.

We evolved to that point but then we lost a lot of ground in the '50s because the boys came home from the war and they needed the jobs, so there was a terrific propaganda campaign on the part of government to get women back into the kitchen and out of the job market. There were government pamphlets telling women to stay home and raise children. So women had children, there was the baby boom and women paid attention to their children and husband and his job. Women were encouraged to be consumers to help the economy.

Life magazine was full of Frigidaire ads.

Right. Men were earning the money and women were choosing what to buy. It wasn't until the '60s that there was any change in the situation. Again, it was partially brought about by a war. But we have not yet reached the point of liberation in terms of the way women are depicted in the media that we had reached in 1940. If you look at women in the movies today, they can't have both a career and a man. I can't think of one movie in the last twenty years in which the woman has both. Of course, I don't either, so maybe that's right. It just shows that we have come a long way, but we have a long way to go.

But hopefully that's changing. Hopefully, children are being brought up today slightly more liberated than the children who were brought up in the '50s. Not enough—not enough to satisfy me. But just the fact that now Mattel puts little girl doctors in their ads for doctor kits as well as little boys. A little girl doesn't automatically get the nurse bag anymore and a boy, the doctor bag.

So society is changing, and as it changes, women are coming out of their shells and they are being comedic in ways they haven't been before. If there are going to be more women doctors and telephone linespeople, there are going to be more women comedians. Gradually, we are making progress.

I still think, though, it's basically a man's world. I'm worried about the fact that in some respects we slipped backwards in the '70s. I saw a show on television the other night that was a great show in terms of sheer absurdity. It's sort of a takeoff on game shows, but it's so close to a real game show that it's hard to see where the parody starts. On the show there's a girl presenter—the dumb blonde. The host will say, "May I have the card, please" and she'll say, "You sure are," as if she's read the cue wrong. She's quite funny, but I thought, "What is this?" If this had been done in 1969 there would have been letters of protest from women's groups, they would have picketed the TV station, there would have been an outcry and the producers would have been scared to run the show that way. But now they can because they figure that the days of protest and bra burning are over and they are not going to encounter any flak.

Might the producers be saying, "Okay, now that women are liberated, we can show dumb blondes, we can do jokes about dumb women, because women will be able to take the joke"?

I'm sure that's the defense they would muster. I don't think it would be valid because I feel, as I said, we have a lot of ground to cover. It's all right for women to make those jokes about themselves, but I don't like to see them coming from the mass media or from what I would consider to be the establishment. I mean, we had a *National Lampoon* cover once with a sexy picture on it that said, "Does Sex Sell Magazines?"

And they sold out every issue?

Yes. It's like when "60 Minutes" does something on child porn. To whom are they appealing? People who say, "Child porn—how shocking! Let me see more!" I think it's the same motivation.

We did a piece on "Saturday Night Live" that I objected to; it was a parody of those network sports battles in which you see lots of tits and ass. We called it the "Network Battle of the Ts and As." It was very funny. It showed just close-up shots of the tits and asses of people like Cheryl Ladd and Lola Falana as they run or ride a bike. You can laugh at it in an enlightened way and say, "This is obviously a brilliant satirical parody of the networks' horrendous attitude that capitalizes on women's bodies in all the jiggle shows." But some of the people will be laughing because it's tits and ass. They're saying, "Let's see more!" And that seems to me to muddy the issue because you are luring people with what you are pretending to object to. You are saying, "Isn't this shocking—want to see more?"

What was the response of women who saw it?

Most of the women in this office felt slightly disturbed by it. I think you should know what your message is, and I think the two guys who wrote the Ts and As skit were getting off on it. I saw them in the editing room and they were going "O-o-o, look at that one!"

So what message are you putting over? I feel that people should know why they are laughing. Women's humor does have a message to it and I think that's right, because we need those messages.

Anything I do usually starts with a feeling of anger. Anger is like the little piece of dirt in the oyster that, hopefully, the pearl forms around. I start by feeling that I'm really pissed off, say, that mindless women are being praised on television by their dominating husbands for having good complexions. I was angered seeing those Ivory soap commercials in which the man says, "I like my wife to look natural. She's been cooped up with me out in the country for the past ten years and she doesn't use makeup, or at least I don't notice it." So I wrote a piece that said, "I'm beautiful but stupid. My husband loves the way I never bother him with my opinions. I use the soap that washes your brain as well as your face." That piece was written about an issue I feel is crucial to women, which is what we were talking about before. Women are allowed to be pretty and charming, but not intelligent, funny or clever. There's always that choice; should I be Phyllis Diller and be ugly but make them laugh, or should I be beautiful and keep my mouth shut?"

So I feel angry first, and then I try to do something about it. I feel that the result of the combination is more interesting than just making people laugh. You should be able to make people laugh anyway, but I'd like to convert them at the same time. I'd like them to think my way or at least come closer to thinking along the lines I do. I'm trying to have an effect on their minds.

People are so afraid of messages it immediately makes you sound like a schoolmarm. But humor and message fit together for me. That's the only way I can work. Not just laughter for laughter's sake—it has to have some point to it, some intelligence.

Do you think that's the impetus behind most women humorists now?

Yes! I think women are in a position where they are trying to change the world. You could say that a lot of the social activism of the '60s has started to flow into comedy. My background at the *National Lampoon* was oriented around political issues too. We were doing comedy during the Vietnam War, and then during Watergate. There was a lot more polarization into camps, there were issues about which you could feel there was a right and a wrong. Now those issues have disappeared and I think that may be one reason why women's humor or comedy is becoming more important—because there *are* issues there that will affect our lives as much as the draft affected men's lives.

Does an issue that has a right and a wrong side lend itself to humor because you can parody either side— there are two extremes you can poke fun at?

You have extremes so you can show the exaggeration of both. You can also find a position for yourself. There was never any question in anyone's mind at the *National Lampoon* that we were all against the war in Vietnam. There was a cohesion of attitude. There were many shades or gradations within that attitude, but nonetheless you could say, "This is ridiculous" and everyone would agree with you. Now I find that it's much harder for many people to take any position. Look at the Arab-Israeli conflict. I find it very difficult to find what side to be on, or even what the sides are.

You certainly don't feel any ambivalence about the women's movement.

Right. As a woman doing humor on issues relating to women, I do have a position, I know what it is, right away. I don't have to say, "Well, let's see, who's the asshole here? Whom am I going to make fun of? The Israelis or the Arabs—which ones are the more stupid?" I can say, "I see what the issue is. Obviously, it's wrong for the woman in the ring around the collar commercials to be foundering in the depths of misery because her husband has a ring around his collar. Why doesn't he wash his own goddamn shirt?" I have strong feelings and a strong position and I know where the humor is coming from.

This is why I think it's a good time for women's humor and a hard time for male humor. I've noticed that the most popular young comedian today in America, Steve Martin, is doing comedy about the failure of comedy. He comes onstage and he does bad jokes that don't work. And people are laughing because the jokes don't work and they are laughing at the pretentiousness and absurdity of the persona he sets forth. They are not laughing about issues. Many people can't remember what he said after his performance. They can remember, "Well, excuse me" and, "I'm just a wild and crazy guy," but not the content of the material. It has no content—it's all form, all stylistics. It's very funny, but what is he saying? There's no point to anything and I'm sorry—excuse me— but I feel there should be some point. I'm reactionary enough to believe in the concept of satire and a satirical tradition. And I guess I'm lucky to have so many targets—all the men in the country.

Suzanne Rand

THIRTY-YEAR-OLD Suzanne Rand wanted to be a gauze stretcher at a local hospital in Illinois when she was twelve, but "got over that." Later, she longed to sing "torchy" ballads in smoky piano bars. Now, as an emerging superstar, she has managed to combine shadings of both aspirations—the innocent and the flamboyant—as the female half of the hot improvisational comedy team Monteith and Rand.

Over scampi and beer in a Manhattan restaurant, Rand looks college casual—a pretty blonde, green-eyed coed in jeans and a pullover. Only a slightly goofy gap between her front teeth breaks her fresh-faced assurance. Suzanne Rand could be the high school prom queen.

In a cab on the way to the NBC studios to tape some sketches for Fred Silverman, Rand pulls out her "good luck" dress, an elegant pink gown she wore for her television debut with partner John Monteith on "The Tonight Show." The sheer dress will later trigger guffaws among the stage crew at the taping, when the floodlights reveal that the prom queen wears no underwear beneath her costume.

37

Suzanne, with John, has appeared in nightclubs and theaters from Boston to Las Vegas, and the team has just completed their first feature film, *Turtle Diary*, for Universal.

–D.C.

How have the folks back home reacted to your sudden fame?

I went to a real small college where everyone knew one another. But when I changed my name from Ekman to Rand nobody knew who I was. My mom sent a letter to the dean of the drama department at my school with all the clippings and reviews of our act. He sent a letter back saying it was required for all drama classes to watch me on Johnny Carson. He wrote, "See what she does? She does that with Shakespeare. She was the funniest Juliet we ever had." I had a tendency to turn any tragedy into a farce.

Were you considered funny as a kid?

I was a cut-up. In one of those high school polls I was voted the most talented, but at that time I was just singing. Although I was considered a discipline problem because I had a big mouth, I always chose to do musicals over comedies.

In your act, there is a suggestion of a sexual relationship with John. Is there one, or do you use that relationship as a basis for your material?

Well, there was never . . . any . . . . I mean, Monty and I were just good friends for a start. One time we got real stoned and toyed with the idea. But I have an adage: Never fuck your friends. If you start out friends and become lovers, a whole new dimension is put on the relationship, and if you break off as lovers, it's difficult to regain the friendship that was once there.

In any close, male-female relationship, tensions de-

velop. **How do you handle anger with Monty when you perform?**

Well, we always make up before we go onstage. We've had fights, but it depends on who's the heaviest. Monty and I never fought before we put the act together and it's stupid to have a friendship break up. I would rather that the team break up than to have the friendship break up.

Do you censor one another?

That happens with 99 percent of our ideas. Monty and I think so differently that I might come up with something and he'll think, yeah it's funny but it's just not something I can do my share of. It's difficult for us to write. I was sitting at home and I got the urge to write, so I sat down and wrote a sketch, a takeoff on that new doll, Baby Wet and Care. That's a doll that you feed milk and it gets a rash on its tush, then the kid is supposed to wipe the rash off with some magic cloth. So I came up with a routine about Baby Leper, in which its legs and arms fall off— assembly required. But I realized that I could only write my half of it. Monty's dialogue was a problem. He would never say what I would have him say. But it's impossible for us to just sit and write down lines. When you have the jokes written down in front of you, you have the opportunity to rewrite, but our humor is based on reacting to the other person. You just can't capture spontaneity on paper.

How do you remember your material then? Do you tape it?

We often tape our stage shows, and whenever we try out a new routine we tape it.

Have you ever wanted to do material that might offend Monty?

Yes, but if either one of us thinks something is tasteless we're real quick to drop it. We have to remember that whatever makes us laugh isn't necessarily what makes the audience laugh. We do a bit that I love, "Paraplegics."

Monty is sitting in a wheelchair and I'm holding on to the back of it and I say, "Gee, honey. I really thought things would be different after the accident and you know, it's our first time out and I actually think it brought us closer together." And Monty says, "I just want to say I think it's wonderful the way you've stood by me since the accident." I say, "Oh honey, I'm your wife—I'll *always* stand by you." And then Monty stands up and I'm in this rigid position. The only way I can stand is by holding on to the back of the wheelchair. And we'd get boos from the audience. So we laugh and say, "Yeah, we hate that one too, but the unions make us do it." If we're gonna hit, we're gonna hit everybody.

How do you view the other women humorists around today?

That's hard. Too many women today still do certain routines just because they're women. What gets me about that kind of thinking is that it almost reinforces the antifeminist view. You need a basis to relate from, but I think women have plenty of other things going for them in humor besides talk about day-old rolls and how their cramps hurt. All that does is reinforce the image that women are confined to a small and limited role in humor.

Suzanne, you seem really aware of your femininity and make your looks work for you in a fascinating way. When you get onstage you wear your pink dress, your hair is pulled back to show your whole face and when you sit down, you pull your skirt up to show your legs. That all seems calculated. Is it?

Yes. I wanna look my best when I'm onstage. I want to look the way I feel and this goes two ways: onstage it's like putting on my best behavior and getting Sunday dressed-up. When I'm offstage, give me jeans and a T-shirt and sunglasses—which is why Monty gets recognized and I don't. But when I get onstage, yeah, I want to look my very best, the way I feel most appealing.

Do you think it helps you get your material across better?

Yes. It's not like, "Oh well, you're so funny looking that naturally you get a laugh." You know there are some people—John Belushi is a perfect example. . . . He's a very funny person. When he walks onstage, you can't help but chuckle because physically he's a funny man. My way of viewing it is, I'm an egotist. I mean, some audiences think, "That's a good-looking girl. I bet he'll do all the funny stuff and she'll just sit there and smile." It's the most fun for me when I can create an initial impression and then start going into my facial expressions and body movements.

Do you like to surprise and shock?

Yeah. I *love* to. That's basically what our humor is—setting the audience up for a punch line that usually is a reversal of what we've been setting up all along. People will think it's gonna end a certain way and we'll do a switch on them. And the reason that usually happens is that Monty and I react to things so differently that we naturally set each other up. We'll never anticipate where the other is going to go. I have a way of approaching a punch line and Monty will deliver the line totally differently. So we surprise each other.

You like to use your physical images, as well as your thinking, to surprise an audience.

I'm always amazed at people who don't put their best foot forward—comics who dress down and put on slinky eyes and all—we work with the bare necessities anyway. I would never wear a bright, sequined, tight dress. I do so many characters that the audience has to believe I'm a freak in dungarees one minute and a society lady the next. So I wear simple clothes, the things I feel comfort-

able in, so I know if I have to do a deep knee bend I won't
be shooting a beaver at half of America.

**Do you think you would have made it as a humorist
without Monty?**

Yes. Eventually. But our humor comes from listening to
the other person and reacting. I need that feedback. I
need that springboard. To be up there by myself, I'd have
to be constantly setting myself up as opposed to getting
signals from Monty. One of the reasons we formed the
team was that I would go around to auditions and I would
always be the wrong "type." People would say to me,
"You read for the ingenue," and I'd say, "No. Let me
read for the second banana." Maybe if I auditioned long
enough, by the time my character lines set into my face I
would make it.

**Did you have any trouble finding work before you
teamed up with Monty?**

That's one thing about the acting profession—they
need actresses as well as actors, so I find it one of the
fairest professions going. You don't really find sexism
unless someone is doing an authentic Shakespearean
comedy at Stratford-on-Avon in which men are doing all
the female roles. I've never felt—okay, maybe in the
technical end of it more women are coming into their
own—but in any play (well, maybe not in *Boys in the
Band*), but in almost any play there's a female role. And
granted, many times playwrights just use women as
furniture, but a lot of the end product is up to the actress.
I don't think you can blame a bad performance totally on
the script. If you have anything going as far as talent is
concerned, you make that scene, that character, work for
you. And you make the most out of the part even if it's
only three lines, "Yes," "No" and "Thank you."

**It sounds as though you harbor a desire to be a
dramatic actress.**

In a play, yeah. Which is what I was trained for. But it's

so much easier if you can present a product to the business end of show business.

Do you and Monty ever strain against one another in a performance?

No. The only time that will happen is in an improv where we'll both get ideas, which is one of the cardinal rules of improv—don't think ahead. Just listen and react. Because if you plan ahead and say, oh yeah, I think I'll go that way, it becomes too one-sided and the improv goes flat. But there have been times we'll come offstage and Monty will say through clenched teeth, "Why did you make me Nixon? I didn't want to be Nixon!" And I'll say, "I'm sorry. It was San Clemente and I just thought. . . ." Sometimes we'll come offstage and say, "Ugh! I just didn't want that to happen at all," but that's really rare.

Would you like to perform on TV more?

I think I would rather do a film first. Monty and I love the stage because we know the stage. Television is real new to us and so are films, so we want to try every medium and see which we prefer. Right now I could say, sure, TV would be fun but we've gotta come up with lots of new material for TV; otherwise, people won't want to see our theater shows. Our material would be so sapped up on TV that two years of really hard work in putting routines together is gone within ten minutes.

Reviewers have repeatedly compared Monteith and Rand to Nichols and May. How do you feel about that?

The comparison is flattering, but I think the reason is because of the way we do our improvs. We're very verbal.

In a sense, we are like Nichols and May in that we try to steer clear of the obvious jokes. We'll take a situation out of life and put a turn on it, as opposed to here's a joke, here's a joke, here's a joke.

Have you studied any other comics?

No. We try not to listen to other comics for fear of unconsciously picking up their style or nuances. But I make an exception for Burns and Allen. I love them. I see other comedians doing *our* stuff, our same basic premise, on TV and I cringe. I think that because of my training I have a good, objective eye. A lot of the comics I've seen have a feeling that what they do is funny, but they don't have an edge on how to present it, whereas Monty and I don't use a director and we basically direct and block all our own things, so we're able to stand back and say, "That didn't feel right. Maybe we should rework it this way." If either of us was the type of actor who needed a director, we'd probably still be on Cape Cod playing clam bars. I see so many new comics around today and I just wanna sit down and give 'em pep talks—because I've learned a whole lot. One thing is that you get your whole premise and you take it to the natural joke. But in order for the thing to stand up, you've got to take it that one step further. I mean, could Hank Aaron have hit all those home runs if he hadn't followed through? No, they would have been doubles—which are good to have, but they aren't as good—or as funny! I wonder with people, why did it strike you as funny? Why did it make you laugh?

What makes you laugh?

I don't know. Wheelchairs and no handicap ramp, things like that. Different things strike me funny. I love words. I love turns of phrases.

You are into the technical end of your craft a great deal, the mechanics as well as the cerebral elements of humor.

Because what I do isn't really set punch lines. Often we have to justify a scene we're doing on levels other than how funny it is. To me, our humor is more like a series of little plays. People have told me they're interested in watching us because every time we create a character duo, it's not so much the jokes in the skit, it's the way those characters relate to each other. And basically the way we're able to relate to each other on stage is in the way we can slip into another character and make it work. I give stand-up comics so much credit. I could just never do it. That to me is the most frightening thing in the world, being up there by yourself, telling jokes.

Why is that? Do you feel an element missing?

No. I would just never want to put myself through that. You see, if I did a stand-up act, I would have to have an invisible sister next to me or someone I could comment to. I guess I do sense a missing element.

Some of your most popular characters are based on life in the late '60s. What was life like for you then?

I was the cut-up from the drama department and Monty was the political radical. So, many of our things that have drug references in them are just patterned after characters we knew who were drug addicts. The funny things that people do under drugs are even funnier if you think they do them all the time. There are certain drugs I don't condone, but I have to try them first. But we have a lot of good pieces we really can't use, but we enjoy doing them. Like "Chinchilla Crepes."

What's that?

This actually came from life. My mother called me and said that a distant relative had died and she had left me a mink coat. I said, "Mom, I don't eat mink. Sorry, I don't want it." At the time that was my philosophy. But after I hung up I thought, what if it had been a chinchilla coat? So I came up with a bit about aging hippies with a family: two kids, Kookie and Kinky. And she runs into a couple, Pekoe and Crystal, with whom they had shared a geodesic. Our characters are Thor and Snooze. And Crystal is wearing a silver fox jacket. I mean, how bogus. And I say, "Crystal, do you eat fox?" And Monty says, "Bingo! Right on! I mean if you eat it, you can wear it. That's what we've always believed, man." Later I'm fixing munchies while we're passing a joint. Monty starts eating and he says, "Snooze, this is great. What is it?" And I say, "Chinchilla crepes. . . . Oh Thor, I got the most dynamite new coat today, you're not gonna believe it. . . ." And that's how I could justify wearing a chinchilla coat.

How did Monteith and Rand break into comedy?

We were real broke and a guy who owns a club, Speakeasy Keith, gave us a chance. He said that we could come in every Monday and it was enough money that we could live through the week, but this was a blues club and blues audiences don't want comedy, they want to cry in their beer wit da blues. So the music would bring 'em down and then there we'd be to bring 'em up again. No one wanted to hear us. They weren't listening. It was discouraging. Monty came offstage and said, "I just can't do this anymore. Let's break this up and get real jobs." And I would say, "Oh Monty, come on—it'll get better." But I had an old man, someone to fall back on. At least I knew I could eat.

Three weeks later we came to New York, signed with our managers and got the gig at the Theater East. And things have been goin' ever since.

Suzanne, do you think of topics and words to describe situations that turn out to be foreign to Monty because he's not as familiar with that female universe?

Sometimes Monty and I will be onstage and one or the other of us will get a laugh on something, and we'll come offstage and the other will say, "Why was that funny?" We were doing "Chinchilla Crepes" for six months before Monty realized that I was setting him up to tell him that I had bought a new coat. He thought the punch line was the idea of the chinchilla crepes themselves. Here we had been doing this scene and it was working and we both had totally different ideas of what the scene was about. That happens a lot, yeah. But sometimes it's all for the best.

What sort of problems do you run into in improvisations?

Nine out of ten times when someone from the audience gives us the bits for an improv we have to be positive. We try to be supportive of one another. After all, the point of an improv is to set your partner up, not knock him down. And I think a lot of times you see things, like Abbott and Costello, where it's the smart guy and the dumb guy. The same person is always getting stomped on. The main thing for us is to make the other person feel good instead of like a turkey—which would be easy to do when you're improvising. We really trust each other. If I'm not thinking funny, I'm convinced that Monty is and he'll come up with something to save the day and vice versa.

It sounds so supportive.

Yeah, and it only took three years of group therapy and one year of est. But it's true, we're really supportive of one another.

Some women say that their humor starts as outrage. They become angry about a topic or a role and they turn it into a parody.

I can't do that. I take my anger too personally. I lose sight of the humor. If I really feel strongly about an injustice, I get up on a soapbox and yell, "AND YOU KNOW WHAT ELSE. . . . ?!" There's no way we can do bureaucratic bits. What I have to do is get far enough away from something that angers me in order to find the humor in it. It's tough because we don't believe in laying messages on the audience. We're real careful not to reinforce bad ideas or stereotypes, but we really don't try to teach the audience too much. Most of our jokes I consider victimless crimes in that we try not to demean or hurt a group or type. Sort of parody without pain.

Who are your role models?

I grew up pretty much surrounded by men. I was Joe-tomboy. I was the only girl on the boys' all-star baseball team. I loved Martha Raye. I also thought she had one of the best pairs of legs goin'. I think Eve Arden's timing is impeccable. I have yet to see her do something that disappoints me. And Lucille Ball. She showed me that you could be pretty and wacky at the same time. My grandma was a real spitfire. She looked like a real grandma, short and round, but she would buy me the sexiest underwear in the world. Until she passed away, I had underwear I'd never worn because it was too risqué. I was on the road once and I was sleeping in this underwear; they were just white nylon jobbies with a little decal on the front that said OFF LIMITS and I was walking to the bathroom in the middle of the night, when I looked down and my crotch was glowing! And I said to my old man, "Spider, are we near a nuclear reactor?"

This decal was one of those things that glows in the dark. *This* from my grandma, who was a strict German lady.

How do you feel about becoming a role model for future comics?

I'm a pretty moral person. I'm not one to go out and start a movement. If I can live my life in the most unhassled way possible and still get what I want to do across, that'd be okay. But I've never really had a sense of "self." I have a certain confidence in how to present myself, but if I had to go into a store and pick out any wardrobe or choose any hairstyle, I never knew what worked for me. My biggest fear was that I would turn out like one of those blonde ladies with the Pekinese faces. I colored my hair from the time I was eleven until I was twenty-four. I wore a padded bra for years. It was a real gas to find out that I could wash my hair, not set it, then go out on stage and still like myself.

Who makes up your audience?

All kinds of people. An old friend from college who had never seen me perform before came to see our show at the Theater East. After the show she said that next to her table of latter-day freaks, there was a couple from Long Island, she with bouffant blue hair and he in a leisure suit and white vinyl shoes. And those two were laughing even harder than my friends. We may have topical humor, but we find that almost everyone can find a point of reference for their own humor in our routines. As I said before, parody without pain.

Stockard Channing

STOCKARD Channing proves to be as energetic, bright and feisty in person as her television and movie performances would indicate. We met in her suite at the St. Regis Hotel in New York during one of her frequent visits from California, this time to portray the French novelist Colette in a dramatic reading and to promote the premiere episode of her television series, "Just Friends." Stockard and David Debin, her husband, are in charge of the show's production and she has the lead role, that of an independent young woman who leaves a staid marriage to a proper Bostonian to live on her own in California. The story is not unlike Stockard's own. Born of affluent parents in New York, brought up by a governess, educated at exclusive schools (Madeira and Radcliffe), she left college to marry an investment analyst and left the marriage to live in a tiny flat and pursue an acting career. Back to Harvard to study drama, another marriage and divorce (to a professor) and a return to life alone, concentrating on her career.

Stockard has played in a wealth of repertory theater productions and first achieved national attention as the zany female lead (opposite Warren Beatty and Jack Nicholson) in *The Fortune*. More comic roles followed—*The Big Bus, The Cheap Detective, Grease* and now, "Just Friends."

–K.B.

Humor is when a character opens up and the audience gets inside. It's a form of intimacy. If you make someone laugh, it's because you make then say, "Oh yes, I'm not alone." They feel that way too. It's a laughter of recognition—my favorite kind.

So the audience is laughing *with* you and not *at* you. You're not the butt of any joke?

Right. Now I'm participating in the creation of a television series and I'm involved with the beginning level of treatment for each episode. I have to say, "This character wouldn't do this" or, "My character wouldn't do that." It's something I haven't done before, so I'm just beginning to have that consciousness of what the *self* is. It's a funny show. I mean, I get laughs. I have timing. I think it's something I was born with. I was lucky that way. I don't really know what it is. You just know when to hit, and it happens. It's an instinct.

Can you now see any influence from when you were a kid—a favorite actress, someone in your family?

You know, it's funny, but I had lunch with my sister today and I'd forgotten that she is amusing. She's not a funny lady—I'm probably funnier than she is—but I think there's a certain cadence there. We didn't have the happiest of childhoods and I think we've both probably developed humor as a kind of defense. If our mother was mad at us, we'd tell each other stories and make each other laugh.

As a way to handle the pain?

Yes, I think that was probably the origin. We had a very strict upbringing. We had a lot of rules and regulations and punishments. My mother was extremely demanding. We had problems, so we would laugh about them. And also, making my mother laugh would get us off the hook. I was sort of the court jester of the family. Also I remember that in school I was not athletic and wasn't very good at competitive sports, so I would be more of a clown. That was how I got my authority and my position. In basketball, I could never do anything but I could make people laugh.

And that was your way of gaining power—through humor?

Yes, I think so. There's respect for people who make you laugh. There always are these articles about men, "What Do You Look For in a Husband?" And they say, "He has to have a sense of humor." What is that? Some people define a sense of humor as a sense of perspective—I think it was Meredith who said that—and I think it's true. Not taking things too seriously, giving them their proper priority. It's a political tool as well. Politicians use it all the time. They make you laugh in a speech and they are literally dealing with power. And power is a strange word. Power often implies control so it can be a negative thing, especially connected to a woman. But I don't think that's true. I just got off the phone with my first husband, whom I hadn't spoken to in years, and he said, "You sound so clear and authoritative!" I wondered, "Is that a crack? Do you like it?" Making that attractive is an interesting task in life. And I think a certain self-possession *is* attractive. Right now I'm in a position of power with the television show—until they kick us off the air. But the process itself is an interesting one, creating the structure of humor and not just performing it.

How are you structuring the central character, the one you play?

I want her to be funny. Not that you laugh at her and not that she is a joke teller. But she's bright and she's funny. I know women who are funny. They make me laugh. They laugh at each other. It's not just girlish giggles. It's anecdotes. It's perception. It's truly humorous. And it's rare to get that up on the screen. My character is direct. If she feels angry about something, she says it. I think a lot of time women have been told that if they are pretty enough, if they get themselves put together enough, maybe they'll get the guy, and that's where they'll get the rent or bread and butter. That is the traditional role for women. To be on his arm and all that—not to be independent. And it's tricky when you start fiddling with that, because it's an ancient concept, and one that I was raised with. So the idea of a woman being funny—I think a lot of men find it appealing but often don't know what to do with it. I find increasingly, however, that there are funny women who are funny with their husbands.

Are you?

My husband is a funny man. He's also a very handsome man. And I remember—now this is a reversal—when I met him—he's got black curly hair and a big black mustache and a very good body—I thought, "Ah, a Laurel Canyon stud," before he opened his mouth. Then he opened his mouth and he made me laugh hysterically and his physicality disappeared, it just disappeared, and I was with this funny man. It wasn't until the second time I was with him that I suddenly looked and thought, "Oh my God, he's gorgeous!" And this was all confusing to me, as a woman, dealing with a man who was funny because we associate funny men with funny-looking men. It runs both ways. It's usually the woman who's going to marry the man and he's going to pay and take care of her. She may decide on a less attractive man, physically, if he's a nice guy and makes her laugh. That's always been supported. It's like a compensatory element.

That's a classic. When someone's first described as having a great sense of humor it usually means the person is not very attractive.

Exactly and it's always been defined as that.

But you're creating a character who is funny *and* attractive and intelligent.

Right. My husband and I laugh like crazy with each other. He's the funniest person I know. He tells stories and I can't stop laughing. It's a wonderful part of our relationship—one of the things I treasure about it. It's where we communicate; it's our exchange. It also gives us our perspective on what we do—we know that if the whole thing collapses tomorrow, we've got each other. We can laugh. We shouldn't go so crazy. So when I'm doing this part I think that if I can do the same thing with this woman, her humor would be a channel, an open communication with the audience. If I had any goals, it would be for the audience to not remember if she's attractive or not. It's not about a woman who is attractive. And it's not about a funny-looking funny person. I'm curious to find out if that can attract an audience. That's what I'm trying to get this character to be. It is a delicate balance, because it's always easy to fall into a certain kind of grotesquerie. And it's also easy to retreat to a situation in which the other people have the jokes and she is the benign, sweet presence with an interesting *reaction* to the humor.

Have you used some of the exchanges you've had with your husband in the script?

No, not really. My husband is not a joke teller, he's more anecdotal and creates little pictures that make me laugh a lot. Humor is a magical, odd thing. Human beings are the only creatures that laugh. It's a mysterious phenomenon, laughter itself. Why do we laugh? I don't know why. It's all been confusing. It's easy to ape a guy being funny because we see so much of it. Especially if you have any kind of mimic sense, you can do an Alan King delivery, a Woody Allen delivery, a Barbra Streisand delivery—an interesting point because she's more in the tradition of a compensatory humorist. I'm talking about her early years.

Using humor to compensate for her looks?

Or for being too smart, you know, apologizing for brains by making people laugh. Lucille Ball had to have crazy red hair and a big red mouth. She was a beautiful woman but there had to be a certain element of distortion.

And Joan Rivers has to have a flat chest.

Joan is compensating in her imagination for being an ex-fatty. She was extremely fat. I played her, in fact, in the television movie she wrote, *The Girl Most Likely To*. It's about a girl who was fat, unattractive, but quite humorous and intelligent. She's in college and she's dumped on by everybody because she's unattractive. She ends up in an automobile accident and has plastic surgery and loses a lot of weight and emerges pretty. It's really a fantasy. What's interesting about it is that she doesn't look the way she did before, but she's exactly the same person inside and she doesn't know what to do with herself. She decides to go back in various disguises and murder everybody who was mean to her. In five killings. It's very, very funny, total black comedy. And people adored it—it's been one of the highest rated movies of the week. Now this is based on a true incident in Joan's life. She was very heavy and she had a blind date. The guy took one look at her and turned around and left. That was it. Years later when she was thin and famous and rich, she was in Beverly Hills and she met the same guy at a cocktail party. He didn't know it was she. To him she was now the famous Joan Rivers—attractive, powerful and charming. And she's sitting there feeling like she could kill him.

Did she?

No, she didn't kill him. Exactly. Instead, she wrote this humorous screenplay. She, I know, is compensating for an old image she has of herself. Maybe that's a bond between men and women humorists. It's not just, "I have a humorous vision of life," but maybe we all do compensate for something, we have a certain sense of self-deprecation.

And the character you're creating—is she compensating for anything?

She's a little bit of everything. I want her to have that freedom. She's not removed. There are some things she's leery of in a girl like way, but at other times she says, "Why not?" and goes and does it. And I like the character because of that. She is not abrasive, not like when I played Rizzo in *Grease*. Rizzo made people laugh. Her character was a tradition—the coquette, the wisecracking maid, the whore, the dark woman. Doing her was easy because of that—my task was to give her other dimensions. What's interesting to me is to take a little bit of the bad woman and a little bit of the pure angel and mix them together and see what happens. I want people to laugh but I don't want this character to be abrasive or to be the daffy idiot.

Do you think the character of Mary Richards in "The Mary Tyler Moore Show" was similar to the one you're creating?

Well, I didn't watch the show often, but when I did I laughed because it was terrifically well done. Her character is not a kind of character that I could play though; it's not my strength. She was definitely a lady in that traditional sense of the word. You never saw her do anything that would be unladylike; part of her humor came from her reactions to things that were off-the-wall. They surrounded her with this world of crazies. I remember when we were writing our pilot, one of the writers was discussing Mary Tyler Moore's show. There's a segment in which she was dressed up in a cockroach costume. They got an enormous amount of mail saying, "How dare you dress our girl like a cockroach!" And that was it for me. If I want to dress up in a bug costume I'll have people say, "Of course she would dress up in a bug costume." It would be awful to be confined in a namby-pamby way.

Weren't you taught to be ladylike by your mother or governess or in private school?

Not really. I went to boarding school and I found there were a lot of funny people there. At Radcliffe and Harvard too. It was a preppie, clublike situation, and I found that humor between men and women was more accepted there than when I was out in the world of business. Nelson Aldrich once wrote an article in the *Atlantic Monthly* that talked about the unisexuality among preppies. I liked that quality because it let you just joke around—last names, you know. When I got into the outside world there were more manners, oddly enough. I found many more barriers between men and women. I think that "unisex" milieu encouraged the difficulty I have relating to sex roles. We all looked the same—wore the same clothes, for God's sake, little madras shorts and Shetland sweaters. It wasn't, you know, like *Grease*. Do Olivia Newton-John and John Travolta look alike? They're not at *all* like each other. They don't wear Bermuda shorts and loafers. That was my experience, but that other experience is probably much more common in this country. This country really encourages this kind of division between the sexes—what little girls do and little boys do. But nobody apologizes for language around me. When I was in school or with friends no one said, "Don't say 'shit' around a girl" because there was no question that you were a lady. Of course you were. But there wasn't a certain kind of petit bourgeois ickyness about it either. So my character is from Boston and the question of ladylikeness does come up, but she's fairly forceful without being abrasive or "Maud"-ish. Now, Maud is a character who had a drop-dead delivery, and that's dangerous, to come to be defined by a certain mannerism.

Do you have any mannerisms that you use to be funny?

I don't know. I was doing a rehearsal and the director said, "Oh, I just did you," and I said, "You did? Let me see!" and I didn't recognize it. But everyone said, "Yeah, you really got her down."

What did he do?

I don't remember. Just read a line in a certain way. And I said, "Uh oh, maybe I'm going to be locked into something."

Well, it's nice to be known for your own style too.

Yes. Woody Allen has a definite rhythm to his delivery. If it happens, it happens and I shouldn't complain about it because it only means that people are trying to define me, because they're watching me and that's nice. But I don't know what it is.

What would you like to be known for?

I'd like to be a character that people can relate to. That probably comes out of my experience in my women's group. I remember people sharing their experiences and that was fascinating. So I think of this person I'm playing as a friend, as someone you would want to hang out with.

Does she encounter and humorize the problems of women?

My focus isn't to create a character that's going to comment zanily on American life. I'm not really a comic like Robin Williams, commenting on society. At the same time, the scripts have been a bit like that. One takes place in a gym, for example, and we went around in tights and it's not a Tits-and-Ass show. And I like that because we're not coy. A woman can be walking around in a leotard and people aren't watching her jiggle. That's interesting because at the same time she's making you laugh and you like looking at her. And on another show she's separated without a divorce and she can't get credit. It's the whole story about how separated women can't get credit.

So you are taking some issues and examining and laughing at them?

Oh yes. Definitely. Not to the wonderful extreme level the "Saturday Night Live" people can get away with because ours is prime time television. And also not like "Mork and Mindy." What Robin Williams is doing has a tradition that goes back to the eighteenth century, to Addison and Steele. I mean it's the Indian that comes to the Court of St. James, the Martian, the Connecticut Yankee in King Arthur's court. Let's not forget when we're talking about humor that everything we're doing has been done before. Sitcoms are no different from commedia dell'arte troupes with the characters we know, the stereotypes.

But you are updating your characters, altering stereotypes so they can be believable today?

I'm being careful that everything we say is true. I'm trying to ground everything in truth so that we don't get quite as bizarre as other people might. Maybe I'm overreacting, but I resist sex roles—women with artifice, say. Let's get rid of that and see what other elements of humor there are, because to me that is more universal.

What about your movie roles?

I've played many different types of funny people. I'm particularly fond of the role in *The Fortune*, Freddie, because I knew why that girl was funny. I loved that character. She had such a great spirit about her. She was positive. No matter what happened in life she was very open and friendly. She was a little hothouse flower, which was what was so adorable. One of my favorite lines was, "Come on, kiddos, are we going to have a good time or not?" I knew, I felt, what that was about. And I did a picture called *The Big Bus*, which I was really not fond of at all because I could not, I did not, *know* who that person was. That was really written as "the girl." And that taught me a lesson—watch out for the white bread parts where they just slap you in the clothes out in the wings. There should be something else.

What about *Grease?*

I enjoyed it. Rizzo was a terrific character. And since I went to plush, snotty boarding schools, people would ask, "How were you able to do Rizzo?" and I said that there's always that girl who had a little clique that scared the devil out of you. I was not that girl in those days, but those girls were powerful. But they were really kids, they were totally adolescent. They always intrigued me because they seemed so grown up, and it was all just a pose and underneath it they were kids like anybody else. And that's what interested me about Rizzo. She embodied adolescent perversity to me—"I refuse to cry. I'll do anything rather than show my softness"—but in the end she does. I enjoyed the part very much. She's also funny, a put-down, the one with the funny wisecrack.

Are you afraid of being typed as a comedienne?

Sure, it's a clear and present danger. That's why I came here to do *Colette*, not for the public, but for myself, so I could know I could still do serious roles. Yes, certainly, people always like to pigeonhole—that's how we cope with the chaos of life. We define people, we limit them in our heads. I catch myself doing it all the time. It's true, as it's true in any other line of work. So you have to show them everything you can do. I'm fearful of that. It would make me unhappy if people started thinking of me as just a funny lady, which they'll probably do anyway.

Eugenie Ross-Leming

IF thirty-two-year-old Eugenie Ross-Leming decided to quit writing and producing sitcoms for Norman Lear's TAT/Tandem Communications, she could be a juggler. She seems to thrive in situations in which she is working on different projects simultaneously. Among other things, Eugenie has done interviews and articles for magazines, she has worked as an actress on the stage and on television, she has written comedy for television, she has anchored the PBS evening news, she has coproduced Lear's hit show "Mary Hartman, Mary Hartman" and, oh yes—she has also fronted a rock band.

When we were looking for women to profile for this book, Eugenie's name was mentioned again and again by people who had either worked with her or knew her by reputation. In meeting her, it's easy to see why her name comes up in the context of women and humor. She is funny, she is beautiful and she has real business savvy.

Eugenie has a solid foundation in humor and the full

backing of Norman Lear, which makes her a powerful lady, even by fickle Hollywood standards. If any one of the three sitcoms she is currently working on hits, Eugenie will be well on her way to becoming a modern mogul.

–D.C.

I understand you began your career in humor as an actress in Second City. . . .

I started out as a *kid* at Second City in workshops, just learning how to improvise and listen and a few basic skills.

Did you enjoy the experience?

Sure did. I started in workshops there when I was a little kid—twelve years old. I basically hung around the streets, watching people like Barbara Harris. The first generation of Second City people really impressed me.

How long did you study there?

I was there in two shifts. The first shift really began when I was in college, which was a drag because I worked at Second City until two in the morning doing social satire and then went to physics class at eight in the morning. They were not compatible lifestyles. So the life of the mind won out for a while and I finished college. When I went back to Second City it was a better experience for me because I was in the company of my contemporaries. In the first company I was in, the people were older than I and had a different sense of humor. The second company had John Belushi, Billy Murray, Brian Murray, Harold Ramis. It was almost like a graduate class. We all share the same reference point.

During your second shift at Second City did you hold a job to support yourself?

Yes. I was writing for magazines, newspapers, I did

interviews for *Playboy* and *Oui*, I was a freelance critic, wrote book and music reviews.

Did you plan to choose one career out of that group?

No. I had this shotgun approach to life. I did PBS nightly news, which was interesting, and then I did some legitimate theater in Chicago, so as to recapture what I'd done in college. I did a lot of commercials. Lots of times they'd hire a couple of Second City people saying, "You're funny—go write a commercial for us." I was part of a group that did commercials and industrial films; writing, acting, producing.

It sounds like it was easy for you to wear all of those hats at once. Was it?

Yes. I'm a firm believer in on-the-job training. I don't recall ever saying that I couldn't do something. Even if I couldn't, I figured I could learn it in the next six hours. Most things are variations on one skill. I can't run a camera yet but I learned how to edit videotape real fast just by watching people.

How did you get to produce "Mary Hartman"?

When I came to L.A. I was miraculously made coproducer of "Mary Hartman" with Brad [Ross-Leming's partner, Brad Buckner].

Was the job a fluke or did you seek it out?

No, I did not seek it out. In fact, I actively resisted it, but my agent said, "Don't be a fool—this is a *job!*"

Why did you resist it?

Because I didn't want a staff job. I didn't want to be working 9:00 to 5:00. Of course, it turned out to be 9:00 to 9:00. Also, I didn't see myself as a writer. I saw myself as a performer. But as producers of "Mary Hartman," we got to do everything: cast the show, edit, it was my own little toy. Of course, a lot of this depended on cooperation and support from Norman Lear, but that was readily given. Brad had done some work at the AFI (American

Film Institute) and between the two of us, we knew the technology and hardware. What we didn't know we asked about. I don't think it's smart to pretend to know stuff you don't, cause people can give you a few pointers and you can learn the rest.

You are one of a handful of "creative female executives" in the television industry. You're a writer, performer, director, casting director, creative consultant. How does the TV community in Hollywood respond to you?

I think people responded not so much to the fact I was a woman, but that I was under thirty. Certainly at this company there are a lot of women in the executive positions—they may not be creative positions, but the women are visible and they're not secretaries.

How old were you when you began coproducing "Mary Hartman"?

Twenty-eight.

How did you feel about the job? Were you pressured?

I thought I was back in college. I felt like every day was another test. I used a ferocious academic approach. My experience at the University of Chicago is probably what got me through this. Every morning Brad and I had to write a "bible" of five scripts a week: what every scene and every character would be like. We had to create a week's worth of material, and a week's worth of "Mary Hartman" material is five weeks' worth of anyone else's material. We approached it like a term paper. We also had to report to Norman Lear for long story sessions. We acted like teachers. I'm sure in both of our minds it was like going in front of the principal. It's awesome working for a legend like Norman Lear (and certainly in our frame of reference he is a comic legend). Brad and I would come into these meetings with papers, notes and pencils and we didn't look cool or hip, you know. These other old-time guys are around taking four-hour lunches and we'd never leave our room. We were probably a real drag to be around because we were so single-minded about this project.

What did that single-mindedness do to your social life?

Pass up the social life. I did not have one. I worked around the clock. Other people would leave and we'd be there in the morning, sleeping on the couches, sleeping on the floor.

How does your sense of humor differ from Brad's?

The difference between us may be as people, not because of our sexual identities. I come from an urban Jewish background, Brad comes from southern California with a much more laid-back background. The differences between us are social, cultural.

Did you ever feel that you had to struggle to get what you wanted, or have things more or less landed in your lap?

There were things I really wanted that I felt I would never get. In high school you want to be—*I* didn't want to be—prom queen. You want to be president of the Latin club or valedictorian. I was very competitive for grades. I was very anxious about being good in school and I wanted to go to the right colleges. Plus I wanted to be a doctor and I wanted to be a movie star. There were a lot of conflicting messages. I always felt that I had the resources to do all of those things, but I didn't know if the world would be fair. Just because I had the capacity, it didn't mean that it was going to happen.

Do you agree with the theory that most comedy springs from personal tragedy?

I think that everybody in the world has some tragedy in his background. Why do some people turn into nuclear physicists and not into comics? I'm sure I had sad things in my background, but I don't think it's any sadder than your background or any sadder than Brad's. I think maybe comics are more dissatisfied and they are more willing to explore other options. They don't buy the status quo so easily.

We were talking about women's humor the other day. Do you think there is such a thing?

I know there's an original women's humor. I think most of it is self-deprecatory to some degree. "I'm fat, my husband won't sleep with me, I get no respect . . . ." Whatever. A lot of times I've heard women writers or comic performers talk about how they were so funny looking they had to compensate with great personalities and being funny. I don't know if I buy that. I think that's a real cliché, even if it's true for some people. I never felt like an ugly duckling or an outcast, and I think that the most beautiful women in the world feel inadequate. The most beautiful guys in the world feel inadequate in some areas. I remember one year in high school, I was voted class wit and most likely to succeed. I was amazed that anyone would bother to do that. I never walked around feeling that I had a Grecian cloud of tragedy hanging over my head. But I always felt that it was more fun to be funny than to be serious. I am a really grim person to be around when I'm not working. I get pretty morbid, so both things balance out.

Do you consider yourself a powerful person?

Personality-wise? I'm fairly assertive. I think I misuse that assertiveness. Sometimes I get hysterical and lose focus. I can be temperamental. I'm not an even-tempered person.

How does that affect your work?

I make a fool of myself often. I say things that I regret or I am really disappointed. I'm trying to get over that this year, and in succeeding I'll be much more cooled out and watch my life unfold without trying to intrude.

How much creative latitude does Norman Lear give you?

On "Mary Hartman" he gave us a lot.

Where do you see humor heading in the television industry?

Television is desperately trying to copy what the film industry is presenting as funny: the disco trip, Animal House ripoffs. . . .

You personally seem to be going off in a more independent direction. For example, your new show, "Highcliff Manor". . . .

Totally Gothic and literate. It may be a failure, but I think that people are ready for intelligent humor. I may be wrong. I think we're going to have a show that has a lot of character reality but is exotic at the same time. The setting is not a living room. I think comedy is definitely moving out of the living room. They may have moved it to the disco dance floor or the frat house. We take it a step further into a Gothic mansion. I think the days of "All in the Family" and "The Jeffersons"—although certainly important shows—are over. I don't want to write that anymore. So I think it's going to be more interesting. The second show we're working on is a contemporary sitcom. It takes place in Alaska. A girl inherits a bar-bordello in the wilderness of Alaska and has a romance with the town sheriff who's the town bachelor. It's not overtly political, but it does have something to do with the individual spirit, leaving the suburbs, leaving the carport, going to Alaska—which is the last virgin land—and it has to do with, if I get high-minded about it, the ecology of the planet. It's the last place that hasn't been turned into a freeway. We went up there and were overwhelmed by it. It's awesome. It won't be about things other TV shows deal with, blue collar shows: how do we pay the rent? how do we send Billy to college? This show is more about how you survive without external luxury when you are your own resource. The whole moral structure in Alaska is much more relaxed too.

When you're here in Los Angeles, miles away from Alaska, how do you keep the material relevant?

It's not about a place, it's about a woman discovering herself, a girl from the suburbs who really tries to find out who she is in a place where that's all you get to do. You have no external stimulation, you can't turn on a TV or run to the drive-in, so you find internal reasons and ways to amuse yourself. The woman in the story has to leap from being an ordinary unmarried female into a pioneer. She has no training for that, or desire, she's just plunked down in the middle of it all. It's a love story, which is fairly timeless. The guy is about ten or fifteen years older than the girl, he's a real macho bozo who has spent all his life being a bachelor—the kind of guy who eats furniture for breakfast—and he gradually falls in love with this emerging woman. The story is basically about how they change each other.

Are you viewed in the Hollywood community as an avant-garde producer?

I am. The networks keep saying [of my work], "This is really amazing, this is really bawdy, this is really ribald, this is really . . . ." They do wax poetic about it. They may not go anywhere, but both shows are different in form and substance. It's not like taking an old story and redecorating it. We care a lot. Brad and I are working on another show and it's even more avant-garde.

Can you tell me about it?

It's called "A Love Affair." It's about two people in their early thirties who did everything they were supposed to do—well, the girl did anyway. They were high school and college sweethearts and then they were separated for a year while he went off to become a member of the Peace Corps and sow his wild oats. Instead, she broke up with him and opted for what she was told was right: a husband and two kids. They meet again ten years later in a small, one-industry town. We wrote the sitcom about the disintegration of her marriage and his live-in relationship with another girl. It's perilous territory because we're not saying adultery is yummy and good and go out and do it, but what we are doing is making the leads of the show adulterers. I suppose the message of the show is that you can make second chances for yourself and that marriage itself isn't bad, but bad marriages are awful and hers is a rotten marriage, a silly marriage, a relationship she entered because her mother told her, "This is what you should do."

So your three shows, "Highcliff Manor," "On Ice" and "A Love Affair" all have female leads. You seem to be picking up where Norman Lear left off—he broke ground in dealing with the family and controversial social issues, and now you will be breaking ground in dealing with women and their emotional growth. Where do you think that growth will lead?

To a better place, I think. There was a time when everybody had to put an emphasis on the social situation: the group, the subculture. Given the prevailing attitudes in the '60s, Norman would explore things like bigots through Archie Bunker; impoverished blacks in "Good Times" or upwardly mobile blacks in "The Jeffersons." The '70s got a little more individualized and now I see that we're finding relationships a fertile area to write about. You can't *not* write about relationships. Women are now more secure about their status, more capable of enduring. They can balance the needs of a personal relationship with those of a career, and TV doesn't have to spend so much time saying that women can be feminine and executives. That was an early '70s thing. Take a show like "Alice." That's about a single woman who's making it on her own with a kid and there was a time for that kind of show. But I think now you can show a woman in a relationship who's making it. Her career is not minimized by the potency of her relationship and her relationship isn't minimized by the potency of her career.

When you're writing these shows do they become autobiographical? Do they parallel your own life, your personal views?

Viewpoint, yes. Some characters can take on a personal tone and quality and you have to watch to avoid that. You can't make everyone a spokesman for your point of view; otherwise, there's no drama. All you've got is a series of propaganda captions and no conflict. I do think that my own sensibilities infiltrate, though. The question of a monogamous relationship is still a perplexing one for me. I don't say it's wrong, I'm just not sure that it's viable. What we're trying to do in these sitcoms is show that nothing is etched in granite and we're just trying to figure things out and keep our sense of humor in the process.

What do you look for when you hire someone for one of your shows?

I look for someone who shares my commitment to the project and shares my vision of it. Brad and I want a team like the one we had for "Mary Hartman," in which you could leave the room and feel that they wouldn't turn it into "The Days of Our Lives." There were a lot of weird people on the staff of "Mary Hartman." We had a boom man who was a story consultant. He came in one day and said that he'd been working on the show for the first season and had some ideas for stories. He pitched some ideas and we gave him a little writing audition and he did really well. No one on the staff was over thirty. There were a couple of people who had more of a track record, but it was an esoteric group of people. That kind of rarefied environment led to a lot of options for the stories. People did not come in with retread tires. They were pretty stretched artistically. You can only get that if you hire people who still have places to stretch, who haven't been doing this job for twenty-two years and are tired of it.

The other day you were telling me a story about actors who come in to audition and call you "honey" and "dear. . . ."

Or "babe" or "love"? It's really boring. You know that an actor is on the line in an audition. At least physically, his body is his instrument when he walks in the door. He knows you're checking him out like a piece of meat, because if he's physically wrong for the part you probably won't consider him even if he's a wonderful actor. All of us as performers are uptight, but it's a really bad opening line when a guy comes in and tells me I'm pretty. I've never walked into a man's office and said, "Hey, you're good looking!" It never occurred to me to be relevant. I would come in and say, "I'd like to work for you, your company." Or, "I read your script, it's great." Or, "I need a job, hire me." I never went in and said, "God! Look at your muscle!" I know people think they're getting points for that. I just turn off; I don't even hear the rest of the conversation. I don't feel that I have a stridently feminist point of view, but I do feel that I should be viewed as a human being who has a service to offer. I'm looking for people who offer compatible services. My day is not enhanced by some guy swaggering in and telling me that I look okay on a scale from one to ten. I don't get angry anymore—I was thinking about it—just amazed, often amused. But it doesn't help the actor. The other side of it is when girls come in and giggle and play dumb. I'm amazed that they think I want them to be empty-headed starlets. It's depressing when women do that. Sometimes Brad will be reading a girl and she'll be giggling to the point that you think she's about to have an attack. It's such a stereotype and you'd think that surely these people are conscious of it.

Do you try to get a message across through your material?

I'm not conscious of it when I write. I don't think Brad

is either. We write off our brains. What gives us energy and adrenalin makes us laugh, and we laugh a lot. I am conscious of sometimes having written something and looking at it and saying, "God, I can't stand behind that. Even though it makes me laugh in the privacy of this room, I don't want to take responsibility for that being public." I've written stuff that's racist, that's sexist—we all laugh at those kinds of jokes sometimes. But I wouldn't want to disseminate that information across the globe because I do feel it's irresponsible. On the other hand, I don't like being dictated to by racial or political groups or sexual groups about what I can and cannot write. I remember, John Belushi and I were doing a scene at Second City one time. It was about aging Bohemians in Paris. It was a parody of that smart Simone de Beauvoir self-satisfied, intellectual, philosophical Bohemian persona that visits the streets and cafes of Paris and ponders great ideas. People who are not always politically involved but who are into pondering. We were improvising, John and I, and somehow I started to play it slightly gay. That was not what the texture and substance of the scene was about, but you get bored and sometimes you add. . . . Anyway, after the show a group of feminists came up to us and they were really hostile. They said we were anti-gay—these are people who were sitting in the front row laughing. I said, "First of all, that was not anti-gay and second of all, not all gays are really nice people." I was doing an eccentric, idiosyncratic character—one person occupying space on the planet. We were not trying to be spokesmen for an entire group. I don't deal in mass movements, I deal in characters. These women had the nerve to imply that although the scene was funny, the consciousness of society was not raised enough for that kind of material to be publicly explored. We could do it in the privacy of our little workshops, and although they were certainly advanced enough to appreciate it, the mass of asshole society out there shouldn't be allowed to experience the ridicule of anyone.

In other words, she was trying to shift some responsibility to you and she was saying that you blew it.

Yeah. It made me feel residual nervousness. We find ourselves censoring ourselves. Sometimes I've written a scene and I think it's just hysterical and then I think that I'm going to be called a racist when it hits the air. We wrote a scene once that some people in the company thought was anti-Semitic. I thought it was great. I'm Jewish, the other two writers were Jewish. I would laugh my ass off, but then I started apologizing for it. Maybe it is anti-Semitic. But I really do write the thing first and then look at it later and occasionally feel that I've gone too far.

Do you have a problem with the network censors?

Yeah. They're funny. Each network has its own *gestalt* and then there are people who side with different shows within the network. I have a letter—I don't know where it is—from the network censor. They're really polite. You're not allowed to use brand names, which was a bedrock aspect of "Mary Hartman." Instead of saying "Have a frozen dinner," say, "Have a *Swanson's* frozen turkey dinner." It helps people. Some jokes work when you say Master Charge; they don't work when you make up a name. Some of these things are negotiable. What they do is go through the script and say, "We've read the script, unload these lines." Then you can go through them and say, "Let's discuss. I'll trade you one of these for one of those."

Do you think the network guidelines are tougher for comedy than for drama?

Yes, because drama's considered a serious exploration of the human condition.

What would you like to be doing in five years?

I'd like to be directing.

Have you done any directing yet?

Not on TV. Brad and I have sort of directed scenes before they get to tape. We'll go down on the set and take turns directing. It's hard to be a good director and really interpret the material, as well as manage the hardware. It's so complicated. You can get really good technicians, but they don't have a clue as to how to tell an actor to get from the door to the table. I think I want to go on and do movies; both of us do. Write and direct them. Brad and I are working on a nightclub act.

Do you see yourself as an empire builder?

I'm hoping for an empire soon. I feel I deserve it.

Judy Pioli Ervin

AT THE age of twenty-eight Judy Pioli Ervin was made one of the producers of television's popular comedy show "Laverne & Shirley." In just a few years she had worked her way up in the industry, starting as an apprentice writer for the brief-running "Sirota's Court," then as a writer for the equally short-lived "Blansky's Beauties," next a brief period producing "Makin' It" and finally a position as head writer for a hit, "Laverne & Shirley."

Judy's entry into TV writing was the result of her once-a-week performances with a comedy improvisation group, Off The Wall. A producer came to see the show, enjoyed Judy and offered her a job. No more working at odd jobs (including one at a falsies factory) to support herself while she polished her comedy. Now it was a full-time job, and more. Her present position keeps her at Paramount Studios up to eighteen hours a day, a time commitment she at times finds difficult to juggle with her commitment to her husband and baby and to her personal projects. She's working on a pilot idea right now, a situation comedy about a young woman with a career who tries to make her marriage successful—and funny.

–K.B.

How did you get where you are at your age?

I knew I wanted to perform as early as grammar school.

Comedy?

I don't know about comedy. I had the first taste of performing when I was about eight years old. We had an organ at home. When company comes over, most kids say, "I don't want to play," but I'd say, "What time is the company getting here? I have two numbers worked out." It was terrible. Up to a certain age I was very, very shy, introverted, and then I just made a turn-around. I tended either to be very shy or else the raging performer, trying to make people laugh and being extroverted, which is probably covering my introverted self. But I started playing the organ and it was a way of entertaining people. I used to make my kid sister hide behind the organ with a bubble maker and I would play Lawrence Welk music and the bubbles would come out. She had to stay back there for two hours and the kid was blue in the face, but we'd get laughs, so basically I knew what I wanted to do.

Were you the "raging performer" with kids your own age, at school?

I had trouble being cast in school plays because of my height. I'm six feet tall and consequently I could only play the mother—you can't play someone's daughter and look down at your mother. My height also helped bring a lot of the humor out. I think you tend to do the joke before it's done on you. If you say, "Ha, ha, I'm tall," chances are it's easier on you than if someone else says, "Ha, ha, you're tall."

Were you the class clown, a funny person, back then?

I was definitely a funny person—in high school too. But I was careful about it. I would only make a joke if I knew the teacher was going to laugh. I was aware of my audience, because I knew if it were the wrong kind of joke I'd get in trouble, but if the teacher laughed, what could they do to me? So I played to the audience carefully. Usually anybody could enjoy the jokes. I wasn't a smart ass and I didn't get in trouble in school.

Did you joke around with just your girl friends, or with the guys too?

And the teacher! Funny is funny, and if a woman is saying something funny or if a man is saying something funny it doesn't matter. Funny is funny and you'll laugh no matter who's saying it. Sometimes, though, people feel threatened when a woman is funny because basically it's aggressive to be funny.

How did you make the transition from organ-playing kid to television producer?

I spent a couple of summers in Vermont playing the organ at a resort hotel. There was a young man, Bart Andrews, at the hotel who wrote sketches and would perform them every Wednesday night. He did them with a waitress who was outgoing, funny and terrific. I was shy—I don't think I said two words to anybody. I was seventeen and it was my first professional job in show business—I was getting paid to play the organ. So one day Bart said, "I don't know what I'm going to do, the waitress isn't here this year," and I'm sitting there eating dinner at the staff table thinking "I want to do this so bad. I could do this. Open your mouth and volunteer. I can't, he'll laugh in my face—I haven't said two words to him!" Finally, I just forced myself to say, "I'll do it" and he said, "What?" and I said, "Oh my God, I'm going to have to say it again." And I said, "I'll do it." He tried to keep a straight face and he said, "Maybe later we'll get together and you can read the stuff." We met that night and just laughed the entire night.

What was his material like?

It was written à la Carol Burnett-type sketches. We'd do maybe eight sketches in one night, interspersed with the guests. There would be a female trumpet player or a little girl playing the piano, and then we would do a sketch. I played a New York cab driver—very sarcastic and put down. We did a sketch in which I played the first woman President. There were all kinds of jokes about my cabinet, the "kitchen cabinet." Not the greatest jokes in the world, but it was a terrific experience. If it had not been for Bart, I would never have pursued the career. It was a dream. I think a lot of people go through life with a dream in the back of their heads but don't really pursue it. And he was the person who said, "Why don't you do it?" And I said, "Sure, I'm gonna become a famous comedian." And he said, "Are there women comedians?" and I said "Yes." "Well, why can't you be one?" "I don't know." "Especially if you don't try, Dumbo—go out there and do something!" So he came out to California with a pilot idea and asked me to do a screen test for it. I left college and came out here and the pilot got canned before I even got to do the screen test. So he told me about a comedy workshop and I was in a comedy improv workshop before I even had an apartment.

Now you had to start originating your *own* comedy material?

Right. And one of the assignments was to write and perform a stand-up routine and I was totally overwhelmed. I said, "No way, I can't do this!" So I called Bart and asked if he would write it with me. He said "Okay. You should do something you're familiar with. You just moved here and are looking for an apartment. How about a looking-for-an-apartment routine?" Well, I wasn't happy with the monologue. I could tell that he was pleased with what we were writing but I said to myself, "This isn't funny!" I got up in front of the class and did the first joke or two and they laughed at one type of thing. Within about thirty seconds I could tell what they were going to laugh at, so I abandoned the entire monologue and improvised the entire act.

What was it about the written jokes that made you not want to use them?

They were too corny. They were too easy. They were too formula. As soon as someone says to a new writer to write something funny, they have a piece of paper and words in front of them and they try to make the humor from words that are on the paper. And they do the most offensive thing which, in my opinion, are word jokes. It's not their fault because they think "writing." I just read a script on speculation, which had a joke in which Laverne has on an electric hair dryer with a bonnet. The doorbell rings, she goes to answer it and Shirley says, "Laverne, you can't answer the door with that hat on." So Laverne says, "Okay, I'll turn it off." Now, I know how they wrote this joke. They thought she has the hat *on*, she's wearing it, and the hair dryer *on*, the electricity. On-off. So they made this joke and it's not funny. If you can get away from the paper, what seems to be funny are, not the words, but the ideas or the pictures. Conceptual humor, things you can relate to, are much funnier than word jokes. And that's what would happen every time I sat down to write. I'd sit at the typewriter and write something and read it and think, "Is that funny?" Now the typewriter doesn't go, "Ah ha ha ha!" Did you ever get in a silly mood one night and think of a thing that's so funny and the next day you tell someone and they look at you blankly? Well, I have a terrible fear: what if I write this thing and I think it's funny and I say it and people look at me like that? If I have someone there while I'm writing, I know if it's funny or not. I find that I write better if I write with somebody else. I think it's because basically I'm a performer, not a writer. If I have another person to work to it's much easier, I have a gauge. Sometimes the other person just has to sit in a room and not even contribute a whole lot, but say, "No, the first one was better." Because I'll give you fourteen different ways to say something and sometimes I don't even know how to control myself. I mean, with improv, I would get up onstage and start talking and people would start laughing even before I could analyze what they were laughing at. I would go in with a character and a set attitude and it would just start happening. But the minute I started writing, improv became more difficult and eventually I had to stop doing it. I was working with an improv group called Off The Wall—Robin Williams is from that group—and I went back to guest with them after a year of being away and I bombed. There are certain things that, if you do them in improv, they are not only not good, they are bad.

Like what?

Like going for a joke. I would get up there and I would try to write on my feet and that's not what improv is.

Did you learn anything in improv that helps you now?

If you go to workshop after workshop, you can learn something. You can polish certain things and you can learn things from talented people, mostly through observation. Some people were clever enough to teach you the things in comedy that can be taught, because there are certainly enough things in comedy that can't be taught.

What are some of the things that can be taught?

A lot of valuable exercises and a lot of things you can be made aware of when you're doing comedy—basic rules in comedy. Something like timing, however, can't be taught. Obviously. I've seen some people in workshops trying to teach people timing. It was amazing. But I think certain things can be taught. Dom DeLuise had a wonderful workshop for a short time. I was doing a scene from "Lovers and Other Strangers" about a married couple. The wife wants to make love with her husband and he isn't interested. She tries to entice him and it leads to a big argument. Dom stopped me in the middle of the argument and said, "When you're arguing, you're arguing like you're doing a comedy argument. You're yelling and he's yelling but I don't get the feeling that you're doing this for real, that you're feeling what you're saying. I think your feelings are hurt but you're playing it like what you're saying is funny. A lot of people laugh when they say something funny—they crack up onstage—and that's because they're not really believing what they're saying, they're watching themselves as an audience and laughing. If you really believe what you're saying, it's not funny. The fact that your husband doesn't want to make love with you is not funny."

So there's more humor when you try to be believable, realistic?

Yes, because when people can look at something and say, "Oh yes, absolutely, that happened to me!" or, "God, I hope that never happens to me," or, "I'm so glad that's not happening to me"—then they'll laugh the most. You can get laughs doing it the other way because, yes, you'll be saying funny things. But when you can really *touch* somebody with that humor, you'll get bigger and better laughs. Reality is very important. I get offended when I watch comedy and the people do something so stupid it's unrealistic. Now, you can be stupid as long as I believe you're really that stupid. But it's when you start to say, "How stupid are they?" that you don't laugh. It makes me angry, and I would think it would make other people angry too. I'm offended when you have to be stupid to be funny.

What sort of women have you tried to make Laverne and Shirley?

I'd like to show them as not stupid so much as vulnerable or inexperienced. If they do something silly or "stupid," it's only because they don't know any better. There's a difference. To a certain extent, you can get away with more on "Laverne & Shirley" because it takes place in 1950 and people tend not to regard these characters as real people. I think that Laverne and Shirley can do things that women today could not. And what we want to do with them is keep them vulnerable, not worldly. Ignorant sometimes—ignorant about social graces, ignorant of what they say. There's a certain crudeness to them because they're fighting, they want to make everything better for themselves. They are not real bright but they're not stupid. They are just inexperienced, poor people, lower-class people. They work best if you put them in a situation in which they get into trouble through no fault of their own, and then make it work for them and get over it. If it's an embarrassing situation, they sit down, realize what's happening and resolve it because of their friendship, because of what their values are.

Would it be any different if they were men?

They have certain dreams, goals and values—am I ever going to get married? What kind of person am I going to marry? Their morals, their friendship as two women. I think it could be just as funny with men. It just would be in different ways. Men can be vulnerable too.

Why do you think "Laverne & Shirley" is such a successful show?

You know, when I started with the show it was "in" not to like it. It was "low-class comedy." The industry doesn't recognize this show as being worth anything. It has never won any kind of award.

But it has consistently been top in the ratings.

Number one. It has been in the top five since it has been on TV. The girls have never won an award. The show has never won an award. It's very "in" to say "'Laverne & Shirley,' harumph! I like '60 Minutes.'" In my opinion, Penny and Cindy are probably the best female comedians in the business. They're wonderful, in different ways.

How are they different?

The type of things Penny does are more along the lines of Lucille Ball in the original "I Love Lucy" show. She'll take something, work on it and find things. You give her a prop and put her in a situation and she'll find things. She's extremely creative, inventive. But sometimes Cindy does certain things, and I'm not laughing at the bits themselves as much as the way she executes them. She'll make me laugh if she runs. It's just the way her body is, it's something uniquely hers. Now Penny can run funny—there's nothing she can't do funny. But there are certain things that only Cindy can do, and certain things only Penny can do.

Did it take you a while to realize these differences before you knew how to write what would be best for each?

Yeah. They are two totally different characters, and it takes a while to sense what's going to work best.

Is it more difficult for a man to write these characters than for you? Are you able to draw from experiences in your own life?

Absolutely. Men can write funny things, as funny as women and vice versa. But there are certain things that men are just not aware of that women do, that women do when they're alone. They have no idea. They can guess, they can make things up that are realistic and sometimes they know from conversations with a woman or living with a woman. But there are things that I and Paula Roth, the other woman writer on the show, could offer simply because we are women. We've been there. But on every job up until "Laverne & Shirley," I've always been the only woman on staff, except for the secretaries.

What was it like to be the only woman?

In general it went pretty well because I've always been more comfortable with men than women.

Do the men turn to you when they need a feminine slant or comment?

Sometimes. But generally speaking, I think until not so long ago a lot of men writers and producers thought there was no advantage in having a woman's point of view. They thought they could write just as well and really didn't need you there. Arthur Silver, who produced "Laverne & Shirley," said a useful thing to me one day. He said, "A year ago if someone told me you need a woman on staff for any show I would have thought, 'No, you don't.' But now I understand how important it is." Which is nice because a lot of times, yes, they do turn to you and ask what a woman does. Or they'll write something you know is incorrect. We did a show in which Laverne wants a certain guy to ask her out. He doesn't, and the writers had her saying, "Why won't you go out with me? Don't you think I'm pretty enough?" something a woman, a girl, would never do, especially this character.

Have you ever suggested a line or situation that the men have felt wasn't believable or funny?

Sure. Sometimes they don't think something is going to get a laugh. And I'll say, "Believe me, this is funny. This will get a laugh, if only from the women." Once I wanted Penny to come out after shaving her legs and do what we've all done when our legs start bleeding—put little pieces of toilet paper on them. I said, "If somebody walks out with toilet paper all over her legs, it's funny." And they said, "What's funny about it? The woman is bleeding!" Well, finally we did it and she walked out with a razor in her hands and toilet paper all over her legs and everybody started laughing. So they began to trust me more.

Was it only the women in the audience who laughed?

No, because men do it on their faces. Anybody who shaves, anybody whose *father* shaves. If you're exposed to it and it's real, it's going to strike you somehow. So you won't always be laughing for the same reason, but usually there are three or four sides to a joke, so you can be the person who has experienced it or the one who says, "Oh God, I've seen that happen."

Do you still write for the show now that you're a producer? What does a producer do?

Being a producer is like having a baby. You take the show from the first step, from pitching the story through all the stages of writing, refining, polishing, improving the jokes. You're there during the performance, checking out the camera shots with the director. Then once the show is shot, you go to the editing rooms and have input on editing the show, dubbing the show, sweetening the show if there's a laugh track. Sometimes a joke has to be done two or three times before it's just right, and by that time the laugh from the audience isn't the same. So you sit in a room with a man and a machine and say, "Make this a medium laugh" and the man presses a couple of buttons and you get a medium laugh on the joke. And if this is not done well. . . . I'm sure you've heard a little nothing joke on a show, followed by an incredible "ha ha ha ha!" and thought, "For what?" It's so obvious it can hurt the show. A producer works out any problems with the cast, works with the budget and has final responsibility for the product. You can work anywhere from fourteen to eighteen hours a day.

What happens when you've reached the end of the day and you have to pitch or improv some jokes? Do you reach a point at which you can treat it like a professional skill or a craft and still be funny?

To a certain extent, it does become a craft. There's a theory that there are only seven or nine basic story lines for situation comedies, and everything is a variation of one of these. For example, there's the bully show, the surprise party, mistaken identities and so on. People who have been writing situation comedy for a long time will say, "So, you're going to do the bully show in that way." It's interesting to think so much of it is formula.

But what happens within that formula when you've been writing for twelve hours straight? What do you do to keep coming up with the jokes to fit into that formula?

I find that to be in this business you have to like to make people laugh and create things that are funny. Sometimes it's very difficult and you go through dry periods where you "ain't got it." There are times when I walk through the door and say, "Boys, you're going to have to carry me today, I ain't got it." So then you play a different role. Maybe you won't come up with the big jokes that day, but you'll sit and say, "No, we can't do that, that's too stupid," or "I think that's too dirty, boys." And you have to be careful because at times, if the joke is funny, the writers can fall in love with it, so you have to be careful of our creative egos and say, "Yes, it's wonderful but it's only a joke for big baseball fans," or, "Yes, some women will know about that but it's so remote—a wrestler from 1943? Believe me, it's big to you guys, but it's nothing to me."

You sound as if you're constantly being the watchdog, presenting the female viewpoint.

Well, I like to think I'm included as one of the boys too. I remember being in a meeting on the first show I worked for and this very, very old comedy writer came in. He started telling these terrible old jokes. He spoke in rhythms and that's all. He looks over, sees me and says, "These are writers? What, you gotta girl? What, they have girls now?" This man was totally taken aback, I mean, comedy writers are referred to as "the boys"—it seems to be a male thing. When people said, "Well, boys" and they included me in it, I felt good. If they said, "Well, boys and lady," then I would have felt I was not being treated equally. I was flattered that I was one of the boys, because "boy" didn't mean someone with a penis, it meant one of the writers and one of the people you depended on. To me it meant I had gained acceptance, I was as good as any guy sitting around the table. I get uncomfortable when I'm not treated as one of the boys, when people start making exceptions for me because I am a woman—if they're afraid something they've said is offensive or whatever. But there was a time I wasn't listened to very much because I wasn't a man. It was pointed out to me once, by a fellow writer. He said, "Does it ever bother you that you'll pitch a joke and nothing happens and a half hour later Bill or whoever will pitch the same joke and everybody will laugh and it will get in?" And I said, "Does that happen? I'll have to watch for it." Sure enough, sometimes that would happen. It is a struggle when you are a woman because when there's pressure, the tendency is to tell the "boys" or give it to the "boys."

Are there more women entering comedy writing now?

Yes and I would say, from my own experience, that it's changing a bit, getting better, because in three years I went from being an apprentice to being a producer and that's a rapid transition. I do think they let me produce because they were in a bind at that time and I was available, but they also knew the quality of my work. However, being a young woman, I don't think I would have been their first choice. There are still battles and you have to fight harder. You do come up against things and you know it's because you're a woman. It's difficult, and more women are trying, but you have to be prepared to fight.

How do you fight it?

You just keep on plugging away, because if you get a little emotional you start to become a dangerous person— "She's an emotional woman" or, "I don't want that crazy lady." You have to gain control and score points in various ways. My best friend Marc Sotkin (the producer of "Laverne & Shirley") was always sympathetic and more than encouraging when it came to my problems. I also found a lot of solace in Paula Roth, the other woman writer on the staff. Sometimes we'd sit in a room and cry, we'd be so upset, they weren't listening to us and we'd have to fight extra hard. You get tired of fighting this battle sometimes. And I couldn't say, "I'm having a hard time, I'm not listened to because I'm a woman" because they would get defensive. Sometimes it's a silent battle you have to fight, so we would get together and talk and cry for a second, and then it would be okay. The bottom line is: Do you want to do this? Is it worth it? And if you answer "Yes," then you have to fight, you have to fight twice as hard, you have to prove yourself. And some of it is self-pressure but some of it *isn't*. You have to be much better than the men because if you're only *just* as good, they're still going to go to the man. But I'm here and five or ten years ago women weren't. Are you willing to do that? My answer is, "Yes!" It's hard and sometimes I think I can't fight this anymore, but the point is there are a lot of other jobs I've had and a lot of other jobs I may have in the future. It could all be gone tomorrow, but I will never be as happy doing anything but this. It's worth it.

Marjorie Gross

MARJORIE Gross hops onto the stage at The Improvisation, one of New York's toughest proving grounds for new comics, her black curls shining in the spotlights. She affects an exasperated pose and says, "New York humidity . . . just *look* what it can do to straight blonde hair. . . ." The audience loves her, and Marjorie is delighted when word filters backstage that two talent scouts from ABC are in the audience and would like to meet her after the show.

Marjorie has developed a stage persona unique in stand-up comedy: she avoids the brash put-down routines so characteristic of comediennes of the past. One of Marjorie's most popular routines depicts two female street gangs: one, the usual gum-popping, knife-wielding kind, the other, a squad of Jewish American Princesses who never quite make it to the rumble because they are out shopping for the right outfit to fight in.

Marjorie's stage character is sharp but innocent, self-assured, but not cocky. In fact, the character is much like Marjorie herself: cute, quick, eager to please and totally likable.

–D.C.

What motivates you to stand up on a stage alone, in front of a whole bunch of people and try to make them laugh?

Well, there's nothing good on TV, so. . . . Really, I don't know what makes me do it. I like the making-people-laugh part and the high that comes when I do a really good set.

Did you pick up any of your comic sense from your family?

Yes. My dad has a wonderful sense of humor. In fact, my whole family does. Zora [Rasmussen] says that I come from a bunch of jokesters. In the family portraits we're all wearing funny hats and false noses.

Did your family encourage you to go into comedy?

Now my dad does. For the longest time, though, it was, "When are you coming back to Toronto?" And in fact, the true test came when the guy who runs Second City in Toronto saw my act and really liked it. My dad said, "Hey, maybe he'll put you in the company." I said, "Dad, I wouldn't want to go into the company now. My act is working and I wouldn't want to break that momentum." And he said, "You're right."

Have you always worked alone, or did you also work in ensembles?

I've always worked alone except for the one time I did a show with a group, and that was an experience. It got me through the winter as far as money was concerned. But it was living hell.

What was the show, and why was it such a bad experience for you?

It was called *Metropolis* and the reason it was so bad was that the producer didn't know what he was doing. He cut out all the good sketches without having them seen by a preview audience. That's what preview audiences are for, right? A couple of sketches I had written were cut, and it affected how much I was in the show. One sketch I wrote with a friend, Jane Ranallo, went like this: The Savage Skulls, a group from the South Bronx, walks into a real estate office:

SKULLS: Eh . . . we saw your ad for da burnt-out tenement. Is it still available?

AGENT: Yeah, but another gang took a look at it dis morning and I think de're seriously interested.

SKULL: Which gang? Who?

AGENT: The Death Rattles.

SKULLS: Awww—dey can't afford nothin' like dis. Ya' got any doors?

AGENT: Nah—ya come and go as ya please.

SKULLS: Any windows?

AGENT: Boarded up. Ya don't have any pets, do ya?

SKULLS: Nah . . . why?

AGENT: It frightens the rats.

SKULLS: Is dere a super on de premises?

AGENT: Yeah . . . he's buried there.

SKULLS: Lets see . . . no windows, no doors, no gas . . . we'll take it!

He cut that before an audience saw it, and the funny thing was, when we read that sketch in rehearsal, everybody was on the floor. And he was on the floor when we first read it too! It's a vaudeville-type of sketch. But he cut it. That day I cried because I was so frustrated. I couldn't reason with him.

Is that a typical male reaction? I mean, most of the comedy clubs are run by men. Have you had any difficulty convincing them to give you a chance?

No. I haven't run into that personally. Some clubs have a more macho attitude than others, but let me tell you what I mean by macho. I mean it in the sense that the guys all hang around together, a core group of guys. And it's hard to penetrate that core, especially if you're a woman. The guys who make up that group are the ones who get onstage most.

Do your male peers get jealous when you're a hit and they bomb?

Not really. I've been lucky in the sense that the guys at The Improv are wonderfully encouraging to me. We help one another out with jokes and sometimes we sit around the bar waiting to go on and we improvise together. Chris Albrecht, who runs The Improv, is amazing. He's one of the reasons it's so good now.

Do you watch other comics or do you rely on your own reactions as a basis for your material?

Ninety percent of what's in my act right now comes from things I've said to other people. I try to write down everything I say to people that makes them laugh. The only thing I saw recently that impressed me—and I was blown away—was Richard Pryor's live-in-concert film. But I don't watch other comics because I become too influenced. For the longest time I had no style of my own. I did everyone else's delivery. I was "The Best of the Improv," but I'm more confident onstage now. I don't censor and edit myself as I used to.

How do you handle hecklers without losing your cool onstage?

When you're working for nothing, you can walk right off the stage. I have gotten hostile back on occasion—and I swear, I *hate* hecklers—but I don't deal with them well. My stage character is not abrasive or rude; I have to step out of character to deal with hecklers and I don't like to do that. But basically, I don't get many hecklers, although women stand-ups seem to attract them. Once I was playing a gig in Ottawa and the people didn't know what to do with me. In a place where comedy is a rarity, a *woman* comic is even more so. Once I thought I was getting a little tough. I was really becoming the fire-breathing stand-up for a while there. Part of it was because I was holding the microphone too much. I put the mike back on the stand and I lost that toughness. It's funny—holding a microphone is like holding a penis. I would lean into the audience and say, "Yeah. Ya know? Right!" Now my character is much more me. In fact, one of the trademarks of my act is that "eee" sound. I draw out the "eee" sounds in "me," "bee," "TV." Like Clara Bow was the "It" girl, I'll be the "E" girl. Those little trademarks are important. Steve Martin built a whole career on "Excuse me."

Do you plan to follow the standard success route for stand-ups: going from the night club to a spot on "The Tonight Show"?

I don't know. The business is turning away from the direction it used to take. It seems now that the route to take is toward a series on TV. People look down on sitcoms, but look what it did for Robin Williams. He never set foot on Carson. People say, "Do five minutes on Carson and you're a star." I think that attitude was encouraged because of Freddie Prinze. He did become a star after a five-minute Carson shot. But that was only because James Komack (producer for "Chico and the Man") happened to be watching that night. I want to get my forty minutes together, get my own TV series and go home.

Do you think that stand-up comedy is good preparation for a sitcom?

Yeah. The best person in a sitcom now is Robin Williams, and he came up doing stand-up. Most people just do a spread in *Vogue* and they get a series. That's the problem with TV. Most comics aren't prepared. In the old days, just think about their training: they did vaudeville 365 days a year. Stand-up makes you develop a *presence* onstage, and that's essential to a performer.

Do you think that men relate to your jokes as well as women do?

Well, I talk about periods and stuff on stage. And I don't think any guy is going to get up onstage and go, "A beeee!" like I do. But I don't write in a gender. I just write what I think is funny. It so happens I thought the period stuff was funny. I have a different outlook on periods, so I wrote about my outlook. Sometimes the audience gets squeamish when I start that routine. They think it is going to get disgusting, but it doesn't. I have this theory that whenever one woman says, "Oh, I think I'm getting my period," another woman will say, "Then I must be getting mine." I call it the Domino Period Theory. All the women in the audience say, "Oh yeah!" I'm telling you, I leave cities and people end up doing my bits. When the women go home and they say, "I think I'm getting my period," they remember my act. I think there's a certain touch to a comedienne's routine that only the women will get.

Do you think the days of self-deprecatory humor are over? Like when Joan Rivers and Phyllis Diller talked about how ugly they were. . . .

I wonder why they had to do that. But then again, Woody Allen does it and so does Rodney Dangerfield. But for a woman to do that now is almost old-fashioned.

Where do you see yourself in, say, three years?

Three, huh? I'll probably be in L.A., unless some unbelievable thing comes up so I can stay here.

Do you have a better chance of making a go of it in comedy out there?

You can make money there. I'm a little sick of this not eating business. The body needs a little nutrition once in a while.

What makes you crack up laughing?

Weirdly enough, as cerebral as my routines are, I like physical stuff and I'm trying to work more of them into my act. I remember one "Saturday Night Live" in which whenever a routine was going badly they would drop a big cow from the ceiling. It was insane. It got so crazy that they started dropping the cow for no reason. I was on the floor, it looked so funny.

Do you write your own material?

Yes. I've also written some comedy for books. I wrote some things for *Titters*. I did a bit called "How To Learn Seating Arrangement in Your Own Home." Also, "The Colonial Sauna Suit"—a device to help your house lose extra rooms; "Fredericks of Hollywood Fashions for the Returning Invalid"; and a little piece called "Facial Foliage."

What would success be for you? When will you know that you've made it?

I'll bet never. You know why? Let's say you go, Ahh! but then you want to do something else. I bet Robin Williams has reached a plateau, right? He's famous and all that, but I bet he wants to make it in film and branch out. You want to try to make a film, you want to try to make records, you want to get some acclaim. That's gotta be the worst word ever. It sounds like when you come off a boat and people throw confetti and shout, "Acclaim!" There's always a different thing you want to make it in; otherwise, boy, you really go nuts. I don't know when I'll sit down and say, "Ahh!" Probably when I'm sitting in some big house. I'll finally be able to say, "Okay, dad. You can stop the checks now."

You tape all of your sets at The Improv. What do you listen for when you play them back?

Low energy, mumbling, my old way of pulling back from the audience when I talk, rushing the routine. I have a habit of talking real fast, so I have to watch that.

Who do you think is your closest competition?

My friend, Lois Bromfield. She moved to California and I haven't seen her in a long time. I really miss her. We used to have such fun at The Improv. People would say,

"Oh, no, not *those* two again." Because we used to really carry on. When I first started out, people said, "Oh . . . a woman doing comedy, a pretty woman doing comedy." And I don't want to sound conceited or anything, but I always knew there was some special quality about my act. Then Lois came along. Lois has gorgeous blonde hair, blue eyes, the ideal American look, right? And she took away my distinction of a pretty woman doing comedy. We've always been good friends, but she's my closest competition. We've talked about it a lot. Chris would put her on before me and that's a real status thing at The Improv—who goes on first. So I told her that I would have to say something to Chris about that. I couldn't let that stay inside. She's on the West Coast now and she recommends me for stuff out there all the time. Lois and I in a sitcom would be great.

Did you think when you were little that you would grow up to be a comedienne?

When I was a kid, about six or seven years old, I was real shy about performing, but I wanted to do it. Lorne Michaels was the drama director at my day camp and we put on a little play. My parents came to see me and my dad kept saying, "Where is she? I don't see her." And my mom said, "She's way in the back, hiding behind the curtain." I used to live next door to a guy who did radio voice-overs, Bernard Cowan, and when I was twelve, he told my folks that I was real good and that they should encourage me to perform. When I went to sleep-away camp, we put on a show, and I did a wonderful thing. I'm still so proud of it. I decided we would act out *Peanuts*. This was before there was that whole group of Charlie Brown cartoon things on TV. I was ten years old. I was such a perfectionist. I directed it, I wrote it, I starred in it (I was Charlie Brown). I have vivid memories of running that whole show. When I was fourteen, we did *Marat-*

Sade. Picture all these little Jewish Princesses and Princes, singing, "Marat, we're poor. . . ." Meanwhile, our dads were paying $800 for that camp. Those were my earliest acting experiences. I always liked to direct the show. I still do.

Marilyn Sokol

MARILYN Sokol is a chameleon. If you've seen her on television talk shows—and she's been on Johnny Carson and Merv Griffin numerous times—you've seen the change. Marilyn starts out the comedienne, recounting absurdities in a quavering voice, eyes opened wide as she pretends she's little Rosarita Farkas. Switch to a microphone and Marilyn beomes a serious chanteuse, delivering moving renditions of sentimental ballads.

The ability to mix comedy and singing, humor and pathos, is Marilyn's professional goal. She has earned kudos in both arenas—winning an Obie Award for her performance in *The Beggar's Opera*, appearing in Shakespeare in the Park and as a regular on television's "Dick van Dyke Show." She's had her own comedy show on radio, helped found The Ace Trucking Company and performed her own act—her unique blend of funning and singing—to SRO audiences across the country.

In films, Marilyn was the neurotic librarian in *Foul Play*, the ascerbic commercial artist in *Something Short of Paradise*, and an upper-middle-class malcontent in *The Last Married Couple in America*.

–K.B.

Some women feel sexual innuendo is hard to deal with successfully. Yet you do so frequently in your talk show appearances. How?

First, I think there is an innocent adjustment I make in order to separate myself from the things I'm saying. It's like "she knows not what she's saying." Innocence is a disclaimer. Also, you can do it if you're not angry. When I go to places like The Improv or The Comedy Store—which I don't go to or perform at very often because those places make me nuts; they're a really harsh world—I've noticed anger in the humor of the women performing when the material is sexually oriented. I don't believe that humor has to come from anger. It can come from pain, it can come from observing people and their idiosyncrasies and things people can identify with, but I don't laugh when it comes from anger. It doesn't seem funny to me. When it comes from anger, it feels self-deprecating. You're saying, "Ugh, this guy did this to me!" and you bother to say it because you're still pissed about it. And I'm thinking, "Tell me something else. That may be so, but I hope you have other life experiences." You don't have to stay angry that way. That's a personal view, but I think a lot of people feel that way. Maybe they call the woman "harsh." They might say, "Oh, she's funny, but she's hard." Or, "She ain't so funny because she's hard." But what she is, basically, is angry and frightened. It makes me feel sorry for her, or wish she could go on past it. Because there's fun in sex, and if it's approached comedically from that point of view, then it's something that's fun and fun to do. That's how I approach it.

When did you start exploring using sex in your material?

I don't explore it consciously. It's just a natural thing. I don't feel that it is a predominant thing in my humor. It's there. It's there in everybody's humor.

For women, though?

Not so much. But I grew up in a household where those kinds of jokes and that point of view were very much there. It came from my mother—she had a bawdy sense of humor. There were more women than men in my family and when we would all get together there would be my sister, myself, my cousin Betty, my Aunt Lillian, my Aunt Mabel, my mother. Of course, there were guys too—the husbands and the male cousins. But even with them it was always, you can't take a shower because cousin Stephen is gonna come up and *somehow* see you, even though the crack between the shower curtains was only an eighth of an inch. So it was very titillating and sexual and humorous.

Were the women in the family the initiators of the humor and the men the ones who reacted?

The men were the worker bees. My father has a different kind of humor—he's a punster. Also, he was quieter than my mother, and he expressed himself more with the piano. So my father was the source of the music. And my sister is very funny. She's a painter, but she said, "Everyday, I'm going to make some funny comment, either an acerbic or satirical comment, about life." So she's doing it every day. That's her discipline.

Is she going to sell them to you?

Naw. Oh, I told her I would buy them, but I'm really intimidated by it, so now I'm going to try to do it too.

You do a lot of characters in your act and on television. What inspires them? Were you like spunky little Rosarita Farkas when you were young?

That's me. The little girl got born when I was with The Ace Trucking Company. She's audacious and her precocious qualities come from a part of me that didn't express them when I was a kid. That's how I would analyze it. I'm not too analytical when it comes to humor.

It just comes about spontaneously and I say, "Yeah, I'd like to do such-and-such a character." Somehow I gravitate to a certain kind of character instinctively and I know that I have to write material for the character. It's never something that's premeditated. I don't say, "Oh, I'm going to satirize so-and-so." I was never very good at imitations. As a kid I imitated Zsa Zsa Gabor—you know, a six-year-old Zsa Zsa—but I never pursued that. That's a particular gift, to be able to imitate, and I believe that it's inside everyone. It's just a matter of getting it out.

Is the use of characters, rather than relying on one-liners in a comedy act, something fairly recent? Jonathan Winters did it. . . .

And Chaplin did it and Buster Keaton and Mae West in the movies. Having characters is a way, certainly, to get away from one-liners. An occasional one-liner can be wonderful, provided it comes from something that's human. If it just exists as a joke and you do a series of them, it wears thin after a while. The character herself is often funny too, so you don't necessarily have to come out with jokes.

When you're acting out a character that someone else has written—in the movie roles you've had, say—how do you make it funny?

It's easier in some ways to do a role, that is, if you believe that it's all inside you. That's the belief that I have. It's a matter of finding out where the similarities are between you and the character. I think everyone who is involved in one or another art form develops a sense of what's true, and you may have a few choices that may all be true for the character. So it's just a matter of choosing in a particular moment which is the most interesting choice and which choice makes you most alive. I find, working as a comedienne, that often you have a choice between making something physically funny or not. In my experience, whenever the physical gets involved, it makes it ten times better, ten times more powerful.

What do you do that's physically funny?

I made an observation when I first started to do the act that I must look elegant—not frilly, but sharp and elegant—so that whatever I do, even if it turns into a pratfall, it's all the more funny because of the way I look.

That contradiction?

Yes, and I was very happy to read that Chaplin told Martha Raye to do that, to look absolutely gorgeous because when she does take a pratfall, she'll only have to trip a little bit because you don't have to fall all the way when you look like a lady.

What are some of the physical gestures you might use to be funny?

I can't really explain it. It's like sitting down and talking about belly dancing, or getting up and actually doing it. If you talk about not being able to bump, it's one thing, but to get up and try and fail, that's another.

You seem to make use of facial expressions.

Facial stuff comes naturally. People have said to me, "You have a rubber face." And they say something about my eyes too. But luckily, I'm not aware of it. And when I see myself on camera, I cringe. I try to learn. I always approach looking at a piece of film or tape objectively and try to be dispassionate and learn, but it's very difficult, not being too hard on yourself.

What usually makes you cringe the most?

What I cringe at is anything that looks dishonest. I will stand behind anything that's gutsy, but when I see myself scared and pulling back, that makes me cringe. You always win when you put yourself out. You know, I saw my last Merv Griffin show, which was just aired, and I was as pleased as could be because I was way out there. It was like my living room. In essence, most people go into comedy because they made their friends and relatives laugh, and the way they made them laugh was either at school or in their bedrooms or living rooms. If you can get that same sense of fun and freedom in front of thousands of people, I think you've gone a long way. We talked on the show and it was spontaneously fun, and then I turned around and sang a serious song, which is what I want to do. I accomplished what I wished to on that show, yet I approached the viewing of it cringing, because I didn't think I had fulfilled it in the studio. Not because of the audience reaction, but because of mine. Sometimes when you think you have done your lousiest performance, it's your best. The reason you feel it was lousy is because you didn't have everything under control. When you don't have controls, sparks come out of you and that, I suppose, is what's called magic. So you have to get some objective opinions when you think you have utterly stunk.

Who is your honest critic? Your manager?

Oh, he's very limited in his compliments. I have two or three good friends who will tell me, and be supportive if they see me going in a direction that's real good, real adventuresome.

What's adventuresome for you?

Grabbing that untrodden territory that either I haven't experienced or haven't seen somebody else do. Can I do that? Gee, it's never been done before—it just might work. I'd rather do something that's never been done before. For instance, when I talked about my first "home run" on "The Tonight Show"—I was using a metaphor for the first time I made it with a guy—I couldn't remember anybody talking about that and I suspected no one had. I was scared to do it but I thought, my goodness, *I* don't think it's terrible. I think it's wonderful. Most everybody out there—it's an adult show—can identify with it, so I'm safe in that. So I trusted the audience.

Of all the things I do, the things that I respect the least are the jokes. I think jokes are the easiest thing to do.

Why do you do them—to get things rolling?

Yes, jokes do that. Also, when you are alone it's real hard not to. When you are improvising, you don't do jokes usually. The lines come naturally and that's when the best stuff occurs. I'm working on a character now and she's jokeless, but I know she's intrinsically funny.

Who's this?

It's Sonja Henjapenja. She's a hostess on a cruise ship and she's wonderful but it's going to take a while before I can really do her and it's going to take a while for the audience to understand what it is I'm doing.

How will you work out Sonja? You don't go to the clubs to test your material.

I work the characters out in my living room, with one or two people. See, I have a built-in problem. I don't work out in public. Even when I did my act here in New York I did an untried act. That sounds like masochism but there was no place I could try it out. There were even economic problems. I had three instruments in back of me and I couldn't afford to go somewhere one night and try it out. There's something also that goes back to my concept of a living room. If you've rehearsed it and you feel it's good, just have faith in that and go out and do it.

How did you come up with the character of Sonja?

I buy an occasional piece of jewelry from a woman I think is Hungarian. She talks in a way that's fascinating to me. I didn't think it was funny, but it was fascinating, and a friend of mine dropped by one time and I started to talk like her and we began to improvise and that's how it happened. That's how I find a lot of the stuff happens, with somebody else, usually a friend. I have a friend, Seth Allen, and he knows how to talk to Rosarita and he knows how to talk to Sonja. But I haven't been doing characters for a while. I've learned that if you are going to sit on a panel on television as I do, and not get up and do stand-up, it's best to do real life stuff. The audience really likes it.

What do you mean by "life stuff"?

The best humor comes from your real life experiences. It's just a matter of selective observation. No jokes, just fairly spontaneous life experiences.

On talk shows, do you know in advance what the host is going to ask?

Well, if you are really there, then you can go with anything. But you pretty much know what is going to be asked, that's discussed up front. But a lot of the time Merv has asked me other things. Flirtation is an important element too.

You flirt with Merv?

Well, one of the strongest parts of what I do is—I'm kind of like a pot that's going to boil over, but I'm holding the lid. Holding the lid is flirting. Now in real life I'm much more direct. But that flirting comes out of a natural excitement of being there. I am excited to be there. And if I'm not excited, if I walk onto a nightclub stage and I'm not excited, well, I think then I'm really sunk. I'd better be excited. You just get excited at the thought that you are going to reveal yourself to all those people.

What's exciting for you now—any new projects?

My fondest wish right now is to do a play, to get back into live theater. I've missed it terribly. I started to do my act basically so that I would have more power in the theater, more power to call shots, more autonomy. The act was my way of having a business—it was my small business.

Why did your act consist of music and stories in a humorous vein rather than music with dramatic recitations?

Because I was funny and I knew I was funny. There were times I would audition for parts and people would laugh when I wasn't trying to make them laugh. I just knew I was funny.

Is it maddening when people do that?

It's all right. It's attention. But as a result of my act I knew I had finally mastered the technique of moving people when I wished to, moving them in a more serious way. The thing that I really got off on was taking them from the serious to the humorous and knowing that I didn't have to make transitions. In other words, if I knew that it was real, everyone else would. I've never heard—except once on television—someone laugh when I started to do a ballad. If I know that it's serious, everybody else understands that. I experienced that and I knew it was possible when I did *The Beggar's Opera* and I portrayed a character who went from being funny to being touching. And I enjoyed it. There's tremendous power in that. Also, it's stimulating, it's like tickling these two diverse parts of yourself and intertwining them. To be able to do that, to make those two parts equally powerful, is a real thrill. There were times when the humor was more powerful than the singing and there were times when the singing was more powerful than the humor. Right now I would guess that people think of me more in terms of being a comedienne. And I think that I've begun to accept it and enjoy it because I know how hard it is to make people laugh. I know it's acting, and there are people who understand that it's acting and that it's not easy. Whether or not they understand that it's acting is, at rock bottom, not important. It's important for me to enjoy if somebody passes me on the street and says, "You're a funny lady." That's what they've seen of me and if I've made them laugh, that's great. When I think of the people who have affected me in the plays I've seen recently, it's been people who have made me laugh. Yet they've also been poignant. That's what I aspire to—that's what Chaplin had. I'm having a television pilot written for me and the character is coming from a very funny place, but I'm talking to the writers about having definite moments of truth and poignancy that make the character more human. I think it will still be predominantly funny, and if it is, hooray! I just think that if you are going to do a half-hour situation comedy on television, it had *better* be funny. And the character I would portray had better be the initiator of the action. I hate it when lead characters are the reactors.

Will the character share any of your qualities?

She's reminiscent of what I described before—a person who is about to burst open but keeping a controlled top. The character is somebody who has a straight job—she's a guidance counselor in a high school in Staten Island—but she's a little crazy. So some of the humor will come from the fine madness that you see, but some of it will also come from how you see her try to fit into this straighter environment. Humor usually comes out of some kind of conflict. She's kind of a fish out of water—you would think of her more in another profession. But there she is, a guidance counselor. People are really multifaceted. There are guidance counselors who are daffy. She's spontaneous, and there are limits on the spontaneity you can express within the confines of a Staten Island high school. And, as I've said, I'd like her to be touching too. It's really terrific to make people laugh and then tug at their heartstrings. And I suppose if I can do that consistently, people would understand that that's what I'm doing. That would be terrific. If I could accomplish that, I think that's an accomplishment of a lifetime.

Deanne Stillman

DEANNE Stillman and I seem to talk simultaneously, which made our interview a bit crazy, but an awful lot of fun. We sat in the kitchen of her New York loft and sipped rum and swapped Cleveland stories (our mutual hometown) for seven hours. As we slowly became punchy from rum and laughter, Deanne showed me photos from her "working vacation" in the Caribbean, where she had been writing the television adaptation of her best-seller, *Titters: The First Collection of Humor by Women*.

Deanne's sense of humor is dry—even acerbic—but you can get her to laugh out loud with the mention of certain words: "spoolie," "dippity-doo," "cuticle," "dress shield." . . . Deanne is a master of detail and nuance and a stickler for written rhythms. Her imagination has been captured by a broad range of topics. Deanne has written articles such as, "Man, God and Johnny Carson," a serious analysis of the religious implications in Johnny Carson's "Tonight Show" monologues, but she really shines when writing humorous pieces, such as her tongue-in-cheek memoir, "I Remember Shoplifting."

117

Deanne is the coauthor of *Woodstock Census: The Nation-wide Survey of the Sixties Generation*, which, according to Abbie Hoffman, is "the only book worth reading on the subject in 1980"; she is a contributor to two anthologies, *American Mass Media* and *Junk Food*. And at the age of twenty-nine, Deanne claims to be at work on her auto-biography, tentatively titled, *Live Like Me*.

–D.C.

Where were you first published?

In New York, in skin mags, although I had been published before that in the underground press. During the '60s and early '70s, the underground press was a place where a lot of people learned everything there is to know about newspaper publishing and reporting and journal-ism and headlines and photo captions and typesetting— all phases of newspaper and magazine production. You could learn everything if you wanted to because the underground newspapers were published by anyone who happened to walk into the office. That attitude accounted for a lot of "typos"—America was usually spelled with fifteen *K*'s instead of one *C*. Anyone who walked into the office and said, "Hey man, can I write some headlines?" was told, "Sure!" I always wanted to write, and it was an ideal experience for me. I really did not want to get a job on the *Cleveland Plain Dealer* or the *Fresno Bee*. I was against that kind of journalism, have been against it, the journalism of the American press which is based on the idea that there are two sides to every story and the truth lies somewhere approximately due north of center.

How did you go about getting published?

I used to send in parodies to *Mad* magazine. I made up parodies of the *Cleveland Plain Dealer* and I did a parody of the *National Enquirer*. I started reading *Mad* religiously when I was eight years old and kept it up through junior high—at which point I started reading *Peyton Place* religiously.

Did *Mad* publish your parodies?

No. I used to study *Mad* carefully and I noticed that only men wrote for the magazine, so I signed my pieces "Dean Stillman." I'm sure they didn't get published because, first of all, the pieces were written in the handwriting of an eight-year-old. Second, it was the humor itself. It was funny in an adolescent way, in a juvenile way, but, of course, even *Mad* is written at the level of an eleven-year-old.

Did the influence of *Mad* push you more toward humor?

I liked *Mad* anyway. It seems to have been the first magazine I reached for. I don't know why. It wasn't because my parents said, "Hey, read this!" I used to send away for a lot of things and maybe it just came in the mail one day and I liked it better than *Reader's Digest*.

When did you come to New York?

I came here in 1968, after graduating from high school.

Did you work right away?

No. I went to NYU, where I spent the next two years majoring in striking and chanting.

Did you write while you went to school?

For school papers and stuff. I wrote a lot of things for myself that were not published. When I left NYU and moved to New Mexico in 1970, I started writing for the underground newspapers.

Were you considered a humorist then?

No. I don't consider myself a humorist now, either. I'm a writer. Humor happens to be my specialty. I think that writers need to have a background in many things, besides knowing how to come up with a gag every three lines and putting a joke at the end of a sentence. That's all mechanics and anybody can learn that.

How did the skin mag editorial view differ from that of the underground press?

The so-called new journalism began in the underground press and then other magazines like *New York* appropriated it and passed it off as a new journalistic style. In a way it was a new style—no typos, several coats of adverbial shellac—but it really originated in the underground press. The writer is part of the story whether he or she wants to admit it or not. That is the kind of attitude I've always had about writing, which doesn't mean starting every article with the pronoun "I," but rather having a point of view that is distinctly your own. Today, most magazines inadvertently encourage writers *not* to have a point of view and to write articles that say, "Here's something weird." This isn't really journalism. It's confetti.

Did you find that skin mags were more open to accepting your stuff than, say, *The Village Voice*?

Oh yes. Skin mags attracted a lot of writers from the underground press because they were sympathetic to them. Today, skin mags are considered sexist, but this was before the women's movement started condemning pornography as sexist. At that time smut was anti-establishment and skin mags were considered a renegade form of publication. They tried to publish writing that other magazines and newspapers wouldn't publish, so I found it much easier to get into those magazines first—*Swank, Genesis, Gallery,* nowadays the three cornerstones of X-rated mindlessness. They were more accessible to new writers with different ideas than, say, *The Village Voice*, which I have also written for, but which follows a kind of fascistic liberal line. If you vary to the right or left of that line, they don't understand it.

Did you ever feel that you should start your own publication so you could write as you please?

In '73 or '74, I founded a magazine called *Bitch,* and that was the first humor magazine for and by women. I published it for six months.

Where did you find the writers for *Bitch?*

I was surprised to find that funny women seemed to be just everywhere. Many of them had not yet been published, partly because they were young, partly because there is a certain kind of writing that people seem to be in awe of and that's humor. It's considered more difficult by editors than other forms of writing.

Also in acting. Comedians are revered by actors.

Yes, the attitude is similar. I'm not sure why, but editors seem to be in awe of humorists. I would go to meet editors (who were male) and they would say things like, "I don't think chicks are funny." I ran into that attitude a lot when I was first starting out. "I don't think chicks are funny." What does that mean? It means that they're worried we're going to laugh at the shirts they're wearing, which is probably true. I think they were afraid that they would be targets. Sometimes they would try to cover it. Instead of saying, "I don't think chicks are funny," they'd say things like, "We don't publish sex-segregated collections of anything." "It's not sex," I'd say, and they'd answer, "We don't publish segregated collections of anything." I'd counter with, "Well, you just published a collection of Portuguese short stories—what is that?" Another line they would often use was, "Humor either works or it doesn't work." I've heard this from many editors. That, to me, has got to be the non sequitur of our time. Waitressing either works or it doesn't work, plumbing either works or it doesn't work. Humor is aggressive by its very nature, and it demands an audience. It's personal. It's judgmental. It's critical. People are threatened by it—even more so when women are doing it. But I think that's starting to change.

Do you find that women have a vocabulary that men

don't understand and therefore can't relate to—like jokes about dress shields, for example?

Dress shields, yes, that's a theory I have. There are joke words that a certain group will automatically identify with. The same way that Johnny Carson uses words like Maalox or prunes or Tidybowl Man—all of those words have to do with middle-aged, disease-fearing people. People laugh at words that remind them of some awkward or funny experience they've had. So when you use a term like "dress shields," you're gonna get a laugh—even if you've never used them. But the fact that people invented dress shields in the first place is funny for women. Somebody actually sat around saying, "Hey, let's sell 'em dress shields. We've sold 'em peds and spoolies—I'm sure they'll buy these useless patches of second-rate cotton and stick them under their arms."

When you moved away from the underground press and skin mags, did you find a different, perhaps more receptive, atmosphere for your work?

No, the atmosphere didn't really change. I think that it changed with the publication of *Titters*. I just got tired of writing for skin magazines, not so much because of the editorial content, which I don't find any more objectionable than most so-called news magazines. I find most magazines basically the same. You can go to a newsstand any time of year, any month, and pick one up and you'll see the same stories over and over: "Houseboat Life in Manhattan" or "The New Apathy." I didn't suddenly have an anti-pornography epiphany; "Hey, these magazines exploit women." I think most magazines exploit everybody. What I did mind was the sort of people running the magazines—their editorial expertise, or lack of it. For some reason, the skin magazine world happens to attract the most insensitive kind of editor. There's one editor who's been on the masthead of every men's magazine for about ten minutes, beginning with the

October, '62 issue of *Argosy*. Publishers think he's a smart guy because he says things like, "Let's get Warren Beatty to interview Diane Keaton."

I suspect that one of the reasons you could flourish in the skin mag world was that you weren't labeling your work as "women's humor."

I still don't. We didn't call *Titters* women's humor. It's humor by women. I write funny stuff and I happen to be a woman. A lot of the pieces I wrote for *Screw* were topical. I did a piece on Henry Kissinger's Middle East Position, a fictitious memoir by a starlet who claims to have had an affair with him and discusses what Henry's really like. In fact, we wanted to reprint it in *Titters*, but the Macmillan lawyers wouldn't let us. They said that you can't make fun of the Secretary of State. You can laugh at everybody else—you could laugh at Lillian Hellman, which I did—but don't laugh at Henry Kissinger.

I write a lot of criticism and satire and parody and one-liners and photo captions and headlines—but no limericks. What I'm getting at is that I don't call it women's humor because that's misleading. I did a piece in *High Times* on dope etiquette. I did a piece called, "The Cry Babies of 60 Minutes," a funny and extremely hard-hitting piece of criticism about that show. I wrote a satirical piece for *More* magazine called "How to Be a Rock Critic in 7 Easy Lessons." The point is, I don't write women's humor any more than Evelyn Waugh or Mark Twain wrote men's humor.

Where do you look for material?

I think about my experience. I think that's what you have to use. You can't use someone else's experiences. You can incorporate their stories into your stories and try to imagine what it would be like, but I don't think that kind of writing or comedy rings true. This is a problem I have with comics who imitate characters who are either unfortunate or deluded. For example, I don't think that bag ladies are particularly funny, intrinsically. A bag lady, a kangaroo and a priest—now *that's* funny. But I would rather see a real bag lady in Grand Central Station than see a comedienne imitate one. I find that kind of slice-of-life pathos patronizing.

We both grew up in Cleveland. The town and its residents are depicted as slow and dull witted, yet a lot of funny people come from there. Do you think that growing up in Cleveland gave you any special slant on the way you look at things?

A lot of comedians come from Ohio. I'm working on a piece now about that for *High Times* called "The Ohio Conspiracy." James Thurber was born there. Bob Hope grew up there, so did Dean Martin, Martin Mull, Fred Willard, Phyllis Diller, Paul Lynde. A lot of Presidents came from Ohio too. As you know, Ohio is called the Buckeye State. Do you know what a buckeye is? It's a *nut*. Most Ohioans don't know what a buckeye is. It never connoted anything to me personally. If you grow up in Florida, the Sunshine State, at least you have some geographical thing to identify with. Most states give you some slogan to identify with. Missouri is the Show Me State. At least that says that it's healthy to be a skeptic, which isn't a bad identity for a state to provide. Even if you have an IQ of 43, if you're from Missouri, you're automatically a skeptic. If you have an IQ of 43 and you're from Ohio, you're a buckeye. That makes for a lot of confusion. When you grow up learning things like your state is first in the production of racing sulkies, cash registers and rubber, you find yourself somewhat dazed. You either stay that way and move to Dayton to test products for the rest of your life, or you leave the state and write about Ohio.

Were you a wise guy in school?

I was definitely a wise guy—when I showed up. I played a lot of tricks on people: passing around notes that said, "At 10:30, throw your books on the floor." I also spent about a year of my life making prank phone calls.

Were you looked on as a leader?

I wasn't at school enough to lead anything. In my senior year I cut class sixty days, which is the most you could cut without flunking. Although I did not "work and play well with others," I got straight A's, except for shorthand—I could never get beyond the notations "ish," "ickle" and "E."

Have you tried writing for any other medium, like TV?

I am starting to do that. I'm working on a *Titters* TV special with Anne Beatts and Rosie Shuster, two writers for "Saturday Night Live." I'm also writing a screenplay, "Where the Girls Were," again with Anne and Judy Jacklin, who designed *Titters*.

How does that compare to writing for magazines?

It's a completely different language. Take a piece like my Lillian Hellman parody. It's about three thousand words long. In this case, I'm parodying a book, a writer, a style, a sensibility. It takes time to do that—three thousand words. You can't do that on TV. Television comedy writing is more skeletal. You've got five minutes and you've got to worry: how will this look? Something that's a great verbal joke may look stupid and not work at all visually. You just don't have time to develop premises.

Do you think that comedy can still break ground on TV?

Yes. A lot more ground. TV is always the last medium to acknowledge change, but I don't think at this point it's a question of breaking new ground. I think it's a question of reexamining what we already have. Now that everything has been made fun of, it's time to reconstruct. Every major institution has been debunked, criticized, ridiculed and torn down. People are skeptical of everything. It's time to take a look at where we've arrived. I think that parody has become an overused form. As much as I love

to do it, it's an easy thing to do. You just take someone
else's style and make fun of it. You don't really have to
come up with your own style. I think that people are
getting tired of television parodies. Television constantly
parodies itself. I tune in Donny and Marie and see them
doing a parody of "All in the Family." I mean, everybody's doing comedy now. Every town has its own little
"Saturday Night Live" type of show. Every high school
probably does a Neil Simon play, which means that
Zabar's consciousness is catching on almost as fast an
angel dust.

You don't like Neil Simon?

I find Upper West Side jokes tiresome; singles jokes,
jokes about the Hamptons. . . . There are obviously a lot
of people who want nothing more than to have their
awkwardness spoofed on the stage. And I hate the word
"spoof," but spoofing is the perfect word for what Neil
Simon does.

**Have you ever encountered any feminist backlash
because of your work?**

When *Bitch* first came out, some feminists were upset
about my using the word "bitch." They felt it was a sexist
term, a derogatory word men use when they refer to a
certain kind of woman. I used it in the sense of bitching,
criticizing, not as in, "Hey—that's a bitchin' car you've
got," but, "Let's sit around and bitch." I felt that it was
beyond the question of sexism. Some people, who obviously have no sense of humor, took it quite seriously
and were offended by its use. Later on, after *Titters* came
out, we ran into a similar reaction from a reviewer over
the word "titters." She didn't like the *double entendre*. The
National Lampoon did a joke ad for *Titters* making up
sequels to the book: "Watch for *Kayuks,* a collection of
humor by Eskimo women, *Sniggers,* a collection of humor
by Negroes." People who take the title seriously and are
offended just miss the point entirely. I understand that

there was a San Francisco chapter of NOW that had to have a vote on whether or not it was okay to laugh at *Titters*. I thought that was great! Having a vote on whether or not something is funny. They ended up voting in favor of humor, which was interesting.

You were one of the founders of Pie Kill, the group that threw pies in deserving faces, right?

Yes, along with Rex Weiner, the Fun Editor of *High Times*, my coauthor on *Woodstock Census* and the man I live with. I don't understand why there's no appropriate word to describe the man you live with. I suppose that's the value of marriage: You know what to call the guy who steals the covers and always leaves the toilet seat up. But anyway, "The Agents of Pie Kill Unlimited" was the actual name. We founded it during the Watergate hearings. We were sitting around watching Donald Segretti testify about dirty tricks and we thought, "Hey, if Nixon's got his band of dirty tricksters, why can't the public have theirs?"

Who threw the first pie?

Mack Sennett threw the first pie.

What was the purpose of Pie Kill?

Anything that shakes up the status quo is useful politically. It's radical. *Titters* was radical in that it challenged popular thought. Today, I think that women have reached the point in their lives and in the women's movement that we can stand back and say, "We've come this far, let's have a good laugh." I think it's necessary to do that. That's what *Titters* was all about. It was not only a good thing to do, a healthy thing to do, but a lucrative thing to do. Not just for me, but for all of the women who worked on the book. *Titters* provided work for more than two hundred women—something few other efforts have.

Deanne, where do you see yourself headed in five years?

Out to get a beer. I don't think that far ahead. I'm not

the Kremlin. I don't have a Five- or Ten-Year Plan. I do have a plan for 1984, though. I'm going to set up a Ministry of Humor. If something isn't funny it will be banned. I'm going to start by banning mimes.

What do you have against mimes?

They're just too sincere.

Gilda Radner

GILDA Radner has one of the "nicest" reputations in show business. People all around her—from "Saturday Night Live" producer Lorne Michaels to her secretary, Mary, to the "Saturday Night" stage crew—relate stories of Radner's personal kindness.

The combination of great talent and a high demand for that talent can, and often does, make pretzels of the biggest stars. Too much public adoration and the expectation that she must always be "on" creates the fear that Gilda could be gobbled up by the clamoring "celebretariat"—a possibility she is aware of.

We spoke in Gilda's NBC office three days before Christmas. She whisked into the room looking very much the New York sophisticate in a beige cashmere suit and matching felt fedora. But when the suit jacket came off, Gilda was wearing a T-shirt that read: HOW TO MAKE CINNAMON TOAST atop her cashmere skirt. The comic contrast is part of her character. In person, she is straightforward and sincere, at once confident and vulnerable as she offers cups of tea and bubble gum while we talk.

It's getting late and people drop by the office to wish Gilda a happy holiday. She's tired and eager to leave, too, but she considers every question, elaborates on her answers for clarity and finally asks her own questions when the prepared list is exhausted.

–D.C.

How did a nice girl like you get into a business like this?

There was no conscious decision to take on humor as a job in my life—except maybe when I was ten years old. I never expected to get paid for it, but I chose it as a way of coping with life. I remember looking in a mirror—I was quite a rotund ten year old—and I thought I was average: I was an average student, I went unnoticed everywhere, and I thought right then to myself that I wasn't going to make it on looks, that people weren't going to talk to me because I looked a certain way, and so I decided to make the comic choice. To view things comically, to opt for the laugh as opposed to anything else. But to end up making a living at it—I don't know how it happened. That was the biggest joke of all!

Did you feel at age ten that you had a natural gift for comedy, or is it something that is learned?

I don't know. I've always been funny, for whatever reason. Is that genetic? I mean, it was reinforced in my family. We weren't told to shut up if we were funny. Now when I trace it back, I'll interview my mother. "Why am I funny? How did this happen?" She'll tell me stories about my grandmother. My maternal grandmother was very funny, could tell a story like nobody else—and she could hardly speak English! So you wonder: Do those things get passed down? I know my dad was real funny and loved to get in front of people and tap his toes or sing songs.

I understand that the character of Emily Litella, the old lady who says, "Never mind," is based on a real woman. Tell me about her.

Her name was Dibby. She raised me and she had a wonderful sense of humor. She used to tell me, "If somebody does something mean to you, you laugh at yourself *first* before anyone else gets a chance to, so then they can't get to you." I grew up the kind of person who, if I woke up with a pimple on my nose, would say, "Hey! I have a pimple on my nose!" before anyone else noticed. Dibby got me to see the side of things that was funny. She was all dithery and used to put things away in the wrong place. I emulated her and we used to pretend that we were old women together.

And now you've made the phrase "Never mind" as popular as Steve Martin's "Excuse me!" Do you worry about becoming typecast as one of your characters?

I think the nature of this job and the people here have not allowed me to. I mean, "Never mind" was starting to come out of my ears. Fortunately, the writers didn't want me to be lashed down, so they wouldn't let me do Emily as much. So now I'm Roseanne Roseannadanna, and for a while I was Baba Wawa. They keep pushing me on to the next thing.

Are all of your characters based on people in your life?

Many of them are. Emily *was* Dibby and "Never mind" and Emily's language is Dibby's. Roseanne has popularized real things about my father. He always said, "It's always something." And a certain sense of humor that is my mother's has also come through in Roseanne. It's only television that's made them, and me, into a product. One of the strangest things to me is when little children look at me and say, "Gilda Radner!" like Scott Towels or Snickers candy, you know what I mean? It's like a brand name to them. They don't know I'm Gilda, I'm me. They see this Gilda Radner, this thing they've seen sold on TV.

Is this what you thought success would be like five years ago?

No. I never thought about it.

What do you think about it now?

When I took the "Saturday Night" job, I did it because it was the next opportunity for me to perform. I never dreamed that what has come along with it would, nor was I prepared for it in any way. It isn't scary, but it's something no one can train you for. There are all different kinds of success, but this in particular, TV success and the recognition that comes with it, takes some readjusting of one's life. You have to make yourself a little less available or you'll go crazy.

You project a strong sense of responsibility toward life. How about your audiences? Do you try to teach attitudes through your characters or routines?

Big mistake in comedy. That's the trouble with fame and comedy and taking on success. You have to be very careful that you don't start taking it too seriously. I feel that I'm a *life* comedienne, my comedy is an observance of life. And so to start observing it too seriously would be the end of it. Which is hard, because when I am interviewed I find that I start making theories about comedy.

Do you like to work through fantasy?

I do my whole life through fantasy. If I had to clean this room right now, because it's a mess, I would put on an outfit and pretend that I was the cleaning lady. I have no technique for performing; I only pretend.

How do you handle competition inside the rep company here at "Saturday Night"?

The wonderful thing about the company is they're all extraordinarily open about competition and hostility.

How do you deal with competition in other professional situations, like Second City?

I tend to back off in competition. I thrive better in love.

In competition, I will slip into the background when I feel it and yet, realistically, it does exist and I have a strong drive to be as good as the best. Del Close, who directs Second City, told me a wonderful story once about a guy who was a runner and planned to run in the Olympics. In the trials, he clocked better than the world record, but when the actual event came, he equaled the best record time, and everyone said, "Why didn't you do better? We knew you could do better." He said, "What I did was far more difficult, which was to equal the best." And I believe that in ensemble work, you can always upstage or be funnier than your fellows—you can stick your finger up your nose, or whatever—but to equal the best of what's going on and to get everyone around you to equal the best is the most exciting part of the work to me. Does that make sense?

Yeah. Your performance can't be too self-centered or you upset the balance of the group.

And comedy is very much a sports event. It's teamwork. Comedians have a strange reality going on because we stand on the stage and wait for laughs. You can do a dramatic part in which you *are* the character. In comedy, you have to be just as dramatic and just as much in character *and* wait for the audience to stop laughing before you can go on.

Are you given directions for developing your own characters? Does a writer come up with the idea, or do you present the writer with your creations?

It happens all whichways—and it's happening all the time. Sometimes the writers will take an idea I have and build in a character they know. Sometimes they will have an idea and the performers will integrate it with their own characters. Sometimes you don't find that character until the minute before you go on. We're in constant communication here and we spend a lot of hours in this office. One of the most wonderful things about working on "Saturday Night" is the intimate relationship between writer and performer. All the writers are stars. Their faces aren't seen, but things come out of a conglomeration of souls and experiences, and it makes me so sad in an interview when they say, "Oh, Gilda this and Gilda that. . . ." when I know it's this joining of spirits that did it. Like, Marilyn [Miller] and I gave birth to "Judy Miller." Alan [Zweibel] and Rosie [Shuster] and I gave birth to "Roseanne Roseannadanna." It's a real collaborative effort. Zweibel and I have almost killed each other developing Roseanne. We write them together, so he and I will sit here and we'll both be Roseanne for *hours.* Or we'll go out to dinner and we'll both be Roseanne. We'll work until the last minute in the show, and when I'm doing her, Zweibel will stand next to the camera, and if he sees me slipping, he'll start to move his hands back and forth in Roseanne's rhythms. It's incredible! It's as though he's coaching me through the thing, and I look into the camera, but I'll see his stupid head bobbing back and forth on the side.

You have said that your career's demands put a strain on your personal and romantic life. How do you gain objectivity for yourself?

It's very difficult, because you definitely need objectivity and family and love and people who knew you before you were Scott Towels. I love it up here at this office because we all know one another from before and we are *unimpressed.*

That's why you can speak honestly when something is good or bad?

Right. That's real important. In any job that is so demanding, it cuts down on your ability to keep your personal life going. But it's a business we're in—that's why it's called show business and not show art. It's a business that takes a lot of energy and time to run, and any man or woman finds it difficult to keep a personal life going. But if you let that slip too much, you can't survive, and it gets harder and harder to find new people who aren't going to be influenced by the "product" of you.

Some of your routines take me back to being a child, like when you play the little kid, Judy Miller, and you put a slip on your head and pretend to be a bride. I remember doing the same thing when I was eight. So there is Gilda who can go from being eight-year-old Judy Miller to eighty-year-old Emily Litella. Who is Gilda in the middle?

I'm a thirty-three-year-old woman. I'm just Gilda. I'm not those characters, yet I am all those people and all those things. I'll be told, "Gilda, you don't have to be funny—relax." But that's me! That's what I've been all my life and if I stopped being that, then I'd really be in trouble.

As I've watched you over the years on "Saturday Night," you have always played off your physical looks, but I've noticed recently that you seem more confident of your physical self. You still do wild pratfalls, but you have also started to play elegant ladies who make just one small, funny gesture—like crossing one eye. . . .

Yeah. I look in the mirror and say, "You know, I'm aging well." I'm starting to look more like my mother and less like a little baby. I see the woman emerging and I'm learning to use that comedically. That's true. That's a nice thing to observe.

Have you ever run into hostility from your male peers because you are so open and funny?

Sure. It always upset me and it still does. But you know, it just won't shut me up. I see that being funny—and being open about it—frightens some men. It frightens some women too.

Why do you think that is?

Because comedy is powerful, and it can seem like a threat to some people. And I just can't shut up sometimes. Sometimes I'll consciously think I'm gonna go somewhere and I'm gonna be quiet when I get there. For example, my girl friend came into New York and we went shopping all day and I bought lots of new clothes. I was going to a party that night and I wore all of the new clothes and I thought to myself, "I'm not gonna tell anyone that these are all new clothes. I'm just going to enjoy them quietly." And then when I got to the party, the first thing out of my mouth was, "Hey! I've got on all new clothes! Look at this—I just bought this today!"

It was like the pimple on your nose. . . .

Yeah! I didn't want anyone to think to themselves, "Are those new clothes?" I just realized: I have such a fear of looking like the fool that I will *play* the fool. It's like the emperor's new clothes. It's like walking outside all naked and not knowing it. If I'm naked, I want to know it. When I was a little girl, my family lived in Florida during the winter. A little boy named Mark, who lived on our street, came by our house one day and yelled from his bike, "Gilda, I saw you outside yesterday in your underwear!" I said, "You did not. . . ." And he kept going, "I saw Gilda in her underwear!" So I went back into the house and I thought, "Oh, God. Did I go outside in my underwear by accident? Did I go insane for a minute and go out the door? Maybe I just walked *by* the door. . . . And I thought, the *horror* if he saw me in my underwear. He convinced me that maybe I *did* do that. And I thought right then—'cause I felt sick in my stomach if he did see me—if I was gonna go outside in my underwear, when I got out there I was gonna yell, "HEY EVERYBODY! I'M OUTSIDE IN MY UNDERWEAR!" so I wouldn't have that sick feeling inside. Maybe it's a disease with me—that fear of being the fool, so becoming the fool.

Have you ever felt the audience slipping away while you were performing?

Yep. I can *hear* them. I can hear if you change the channel in your house. I get louder. I just try to make a lot of energy to attract them. Lorne has called me "Kamikaze Radner" because I'll go for a suicide attempt if I feel I'm losing the audience. By the way, that's my only comedy rule: If I feel I'm boring the audience, I *do* something to stop it. I'm petrified of boring anybody.

Do you see fewer lines being drawn between "men's humor" and "women's humor"?

All that's gonna happen in comedy, thank God, is exactly what's gonna happen in the world. Because it's a mirror of what's going on. Women are doing more of everything, and comedy reflects that. Ten years ago it wouldn't have been funny to see a woman playing a doctor because there weren't that many women doctors. Now, it's gonna be however the world changes—as opposed to changing the world. Like Chevy did President Ford and Danny did Carter. Well, if there is a woman President in ten years, Laraine or Jane or I will parody her. We gotta take what's happening and make the comic choice. Here's the other thing I should say—I'm so glad I'm a woman. I love it. I wouldn't be any other gender under the sun. I realize now there is something emerging in all of us that has less of a gender. But it's hard to molt that skin into this new thing—whatever it is. It's hard on women our age, and men too. I'm confused twenty-four hours a day.

What's next for you? Would you consider doing things outside of "Saturday Night"?

That's just what I'm going to try now. I'm going to make a comedy album and I'm going to do it live from a show I did all by myself. I made a major breakthrough when I did Candy Slice, the punk rock star. I had to sing all by myself, so now I'm less afraid. I intend to trick and scare myself to death for the rest of my life. I plan to do everything that frightens me. The thought of doing a movie scares me to death, so I want to try that. So if you'll excuse me now, I'm going to go make a comedy album and I'll be right back.

Lynn Roth

AT thirty, Lynn Roth is the director of comedy development for 20th Century-Fox, the executive who approves or rejects pilot ideas for future situation comedies. In her effort to bring fresh ideas to television, Lynn started a comedy writers' workshop, culling the country for new writers whose thinking had not yet become formulized by the system.

A former comedy writer whose credits include "All in the Family," "Love American Style," and "Hot L Baltimore," Lynn is a pro in the business—one who pursues quality as a goal. She's concerned about the presentation of women on television and pushes for shows that feature female characters who are independent, bright, assertive, attractive, funny—adjectives that could describe Lynn herself. Add to that tall, pretty, vivacious and possessor of a warm laugh that follows her frequent tongue-in-cheek statements.

Lynn and I met in her office at 20th Century-Fox. She bypassed her huge desk, piled with manuscripts, and headed for the couches and coffee table that form the sitting area, the area where she usually meets with writers to hear their story ideas and come up with characters and plots. Lynn had altered the standard executive furnishings by bringing in bright flowers, Mexican wall prints and favorite mementos to warm the atmosphere.

–K.B.

You're overseeing ten new comedy writers—eight men and two women. Have you noticed any differences in their work?

Not really, though I do see a male-female difference when somebody here assigns a project. If the project has to do with an ovarian cyst or breast cancer or love or a famous woman, they'll seek out a woman to do it. When it has to do with economics, the military or government, they'll go for a man.

Did more women apply to the workshop than you expected?

I feel bad there are only two women, but we selected the people from four thousand submissions. First I had a group of readers go through the material and told them, "Do not look at names and don't look at addresses; we're not going to try to find people who are minorities or women or from certain parts of the country. Just read the material." So it turned out that the best material came from these ten people, and unfortunately, there were only two women.

I understand that many people will write a script for one of their favorite shows and send it in. From what you've just said about only ten people out of four thousand having potential talent, that seems like such a long shot.

It happens, though. If a new writer sends in a script, it's really got to be something that sparks somebody—that's how good it has to be. But if it's not bought for that show, then it's a sample of their work and somebody else might read it. I found a writing team that way. Two women wrote a spec script and somebody sent it to me and I absolutely loved it and gave them an assignment on a show we had here.

Are they still writing?

Oh yeah, they're now on the staff of "The Mary Tyler Moore Variety Show."

Why aren't there more women writing comedy?

It has changed. When I first began to write comedy about seven years ago, there was some amazement because I write hard jokes. Do you know what hard jokes mean? They're punchers, they're real rim shots. I write jokes like that, and it was hard for the producers (who were men) to transcend the usual image of the comedy writer which was, you know, some guy who started his day in a delicatessen and then complained about his wife and kids and smoked a cigar and put everything down. But there was a different type of comedy writer coming up, and God knows, there are women who are tremendously successful in this field now.

Did your hard jokes sound as if they were written by that man with the cigar or did they reflect, in subject matter or vocabulary, the fact that you are female?

Well, I don't use words like "broad," "bimbo" or "tomato." I won't use any of those words in my jokes, but I've collaborated with men and if you went through the jokes, I don't think you'd be able to tell which joke came from me and which from the man. A joke is a joke is a joke.

Do you do most of your writing in collaboration?

I've done both. Sometimes I prefer collaboration and at other times I prefer writing alone. It depends on the situation. Collaborating can be wonderful because it is the ultimate union of two people. When you're building to your joke there is such unison. It's absolutely thrilling. And at other times it's like two people trying to thread one needle at the same time—it's excruciating. Writing comedy is difficult. There's a joke among comedy writers that it's so much more difficult to write comedy than it is to write drama. The dramatic writers don't understand this. We're constantly putting pieces of paper in a typewriter saying, "Is this funny enough?" And what do dramatic writers do? They must look at the paper and say, "Is this boring enough?"

How do you tell if it's funny enough?

You just hope to God that your instincts are good.

Do you try out your jokes on others?

You really can't because sometimes they're out of context, and the really good jokes come from the situation.

You say you don't use words like "broad" or "bimbo." Does that attitude, that concern about the image of women, extend beyond words?

I do try to incorporate some women's ideas in the half-hour situation comedies. I desperately wanted to do a show about a woman who is more successful than a man. I wanted to look at the whole relationship: when they met, the courtship, the marriage, the divorce or separation, the coming back together. I mean, it could go on for years. I loved it because to me, that's a real problem today. I can't think of a day that goes by that one of my girl friends doesn't call and say either, "He doesn't have any money" or, "He's ten years younger than I am—what am I going to do?" And I just love that, it seems so contemporary. But I couldn't get the networks to buy it.

Why? Because the people who decide if a show will get through are mostly men?

Hmmm. I do think that. Men are still in control and they still don't know what to do with us. Did you ever see a show that ran for a short time on television about a young woman in a network who was just working her way up and dealing with all the bureaucrats and the system? I loved that character; she was a strong woman. She had to say to her boyfriend, "I will re-edit the tape and I'll be up all night. If you don't like it, go to the party without me." She was strong and sexy and bright. Unfortunately, the show got very soapy and it was taken off the air, but I think the network was anxious to get that show off. They *had* to put it on because people would say, "Ah ha! The truth about networks—you see, they wouldn't put it on." But they didn't give it tremendous promotion and it died a whimpering death.

Were they afraid of losing advertisers?

I think so. I think that they say, "Well, it's not only men who are afraid of women like that, it's also the women." Women don't want to see female characters whose lives are so different from theirs.

So the woman who is going to go out and buy the detergent or the products that are paying for the show is not going to want to see a character doing what she never did?

Yes. They themselves are intimidated by those kinds of women. I was in the South last month and talked to women there who said exactly that, that this new assertiveness is scaring them. I feel they don't know what's happening. Most of the time they try to block out the fact that it's happening. Men are going to have to have their own revolution to come to us, now that we're different. It's like in any marriage, when one person drastically changes, the other has got to make some kind of change. And there's no stopping it—there are going to be women in every single field, unless something terrible happens.

Do you think that humor is a way of overcoming that intimidation, of coaxing others into liking and accepting you?

I think humor makes it even more difficult for a successful woman. If you've been in situations where the woman is funny and the man is not, then the woman inevitably commands the attention—at a dinner party, with the relatives, wherever. It's a certain power, and a lot of men don't deal well with it. They'll like somebody *else's* wife or girl friend to be funny, but they want boring. Or dumb, I mean, look at "Three's Company." I cannot stand it, I can't stand the way those women parade themselves, the jokes they make. I think powerful women are attractive. Power doesn't have to mean they're running a corporation. Power is a strong, multifaceted human being. Jane Fonda, to me, is a most interesting woman and is setting a good example. And in order to bring that into comedy, we're going to have to find a way to show a humorous woman who is not a jerk or a dumb sex symbol.

Have you suggested to the ten people in the workshop that they develop a show featuring a woman along these lines?

I think these writers all share my feeling and we've had a lot of discussions about it—not only about the image of women, but about quality in general. You know, it might take us a while to sell something, but that's okay because let's come up with something good, let's not come up with something derivative and let's not just *shlupp* something together that's only going to last thirteen weeks anyway. Let's fail *well*.

What are some of the guidelines you give for turning an idea for a show into a funny idea?

That's hard. That's almost the question of what makes things funny. Why do we laugh at the things we do? I think that if you start with interesting people in an interesting situation, then every time you examine any predicament, you just look at it this way, you know, with your head slightly cocked rather than straight on. I guess that's the difference between comedy and drama—the interpretation. Step back and look at it from a different angle, and then you have comedy. If it's the wrong angle, it's bad comedy. I don't know; what makes us laugh is such a magical thing.

Who in the field makes *you* laugh?

Woody Allen. I *love* Woody Allen. I think he's a genius. *Annie Hall* is my favorite kind of humor with the most satisfying laughter because it has to do with life. There are different kinds of laughter, but that's my favorite because there's something you can take away with you.

What sort of humor writer are you?

I think that as a writer, I'm probably best in relationships between men and women. I like satire also. But just the way people talk to each other is what I'm interested in the most. I think that's funny. I love to eavesdrop on conversations. I would peek into people's windows my whole life if I could. I love to observe people.

And they later appear on TV, modified by your having cocked your head at a certain angle?

It always goes through my own mental machinations. I don't know, I don't want to typecast myself as a comedy writer with a particular style. I mean, I wrote a very serious play and there's humor in it, a different kind of humor from the kind I ever wrote before—social comment—and I don't even know where it came from.

What's the play about?

It's about the life of Sigmund Freud. Now he has written mounds about humor and what makes us laugh.

Do you find it valid?

Oh, I find some of it *so* valid. You have no idea that such a little thing as laughter has so many psychological implications. A lot of what he says is fascinating—that laughter covers up nervousness. I have a girl friend who's a comedy writer and she used humor to mask her nervousness. She was incredibly shy, but nobody believed it because she would make people scream with laughter. She would use humor to cover being too embarrassed to say, "Hello, my name is so-and-so and I can't think of anything to talk about."

What do you use humor for?

To express myself. I've always expressed myself through humor and I didn't even realize it because I wasn't headed toward being a writer. But I always kept a diary and it was always funny. I mean, whom was I writing for? I was writing for myself, unless I believed that somebody was going to find that diary and publish it. My diaries are a riot.

Are they going to become a new situation comedy?

I don't think television is ready for that. I guess my first experience with humor came when I was about four years old in New York. My father is a rabbi and we were at services when one of the bratty boys in Hebrew school told me to yell "shit" in the middle of my father's sermon. I did, and I got my first laugh. I was addicted after that.

Did your father laugh too?

Yes, absolutely.

Did your parents encourage you to continue being funny?

Oh yes. After dinner we'd sit around and do *shtick*. We would do imitations and impressions of each other and of people we knew. There was great satisfaction out of making people laugh, especially my father.

Why especially your father? Was it harder to get him to laugh?

No, I was just crazy about him. I'm still crazy about him. Ah ha! The root to everything! I found a passage in one of my diaries, written when I was about eight, which says, "I made my daddy laugh. His laugh makes me so happy." Oh God. But my whole family always used humor. I guess I didn't realize that until recently when my grandfather passed away. I thought, "Oh no, there's going to be a bunch of Jews hitting their breasts and sobbing." There was crying, but afterwards, we sat around, told funny stories. It brings us closer together—mutual laughter makes us close. The friends you love the most are the ones you laugh with.

So your humor stemmed from a feeling of closeness, and perhaps from the attention you received?

I'm sure that has a lot to do with it. Also, I was smart at school and to beg forgiveness from the other kids I would make them laugh. That would be a way not to make them hate me.

And to compensate for your attractiveness?

Thank you, but I still feel like I'm going through the awkward years. I don't think of myself as attractive. That's not the first thing I think about when I wake up in the morning—that this is going to be a wonderful day because I'm pretty. But I would say that in the case of a lot of the people I knew, many of them were unattractive and they used humor to be accepted, to make themselves lovable.

Would that be true of men too?

I think so. You find a lot of creepy, nutty, fat male comedy writers.

How did you break into the field?

It was a fluke, like so much of what's happened in my life. I was going to college and I desperately wanted to be an actress. I met a writer and we became very friendly. He was getting over a marriage and I was getting over a relationship. *Our* relationship was we'd play Scrabble and sigh a lot. One night he was supposed to meet with another writer to come up with ideas for "All in the Family," but somebody fixed him up with a blonde, so he was going to cancel the meeting. I don't know what possessed me, just one of those moments of fate, but I tapped him on the shoulder and said, "I'll go in your place." So he said to the other writer, "I'm sending over a young woman with a wild imagination." The other writer thinks he's being set up on a blind date but I'm really going to go pitch an idea.

Cut to the other writer's house and he's playing Chopin on the piano with an ascot around his neck, no shit, and I tell him my idea. He says, "That's terrible" and writes it down. The next day he sells it to Norman Lear, without giving me any credit. So, after the script was done, Norman Lear said, "This is a very good script, let's talk about another one." At that point he brought me in and said, "There's been a writer in the closet and I think you should meet her." So I became a comedy writer. Those were great days—I couldn't believe it was happening. I went from one show to another, until I found out I was being considered for this job. My immediate reaction was the Groucho Marx reaction: I'd never go to a studio that wants me. What's wrong with this studio? When they offered me the job I said, "I'll let you know in a few hours. I have to go call my friend." I went home and called thirty people, people I haven't talked to in years, just to get their opinions, because I knew this was going to change my life. But as a writer, I wanted to see what it was like on the other side of the desk. I also believed a year and a half ago that I could bring in these great comedy ideas and the network would say, "That's fabulous, go ahead!"

But you have to get that fabulous idea past twenty people before it will be accepted?

Yes, and a lot of the things I wanted to experiment with have been turned down, so I feel a little beaten. But I keep plugging away. I'm glad I took this job, though, it's absolutely fascinating.

Is being a woman an advantage or disadvantage?

In the beginning, it was a disadvantage, but, yes, I guess I've reaped some of the benefits of the "Keeping an eye out for a woman, let's hire a woman" thinking, which started in the early '70s, when the pressure began. And I think just now, too, men are thinking twice before they write a woman character. Then again, I've been amazed at women who've brought in Tits-and-Ass ideas.

Have they gone anywhere?

Not from this office, they haven't. I hate that. I couldn't believe that started to happen. I couldn't believe that the Women's Movement did not stand up and scream bloody murder, because "Three's Company" puts us back ten years. My general theory is that sex is out. This whole thing with men and women has almost killed sex totally. It doesn't seem to be as lustful as it used to be, so that all that titillation and all those references on the show make it look as though it's still going on. It's almost vicarious: it's like the guys in high school who always made those jokes were the ones who were never getting any. They had never had a sexual experience.

Why do women bring in tits-and-ass ideas—because they think they're commercial?

Commercial, yes—they want to get on the air. You can't blame them. A nice way to look at it would be, yeah, they'd get on the air and they'd be women in power and eventually they wouldn't have to do shows like that. I don't know, it's bad to start like that. If you're already creating an image for yourself, it's hard to break from it.

Do you find there are more ideas for absurd shows, following the success of "Mork and Mindy"? Is that going to be a trend?

A trend, yes. It's what the networks are calling—I love this language—hard concepts. That's like a bionic squirrel, a transvestite from Mars, you know, your average, run-of-the-mill characters.

There has always been a good representation of women performing comedy on television, but why do you think there aren't more women performing in clubs, doing stand-up?

There might be something involved with femininity.

It's hard to hold on to whatever the hell femininity is and to get up there and do stand-up. Joan Rivers and Phyllis Diller are not feminine when they're doing that, at least I don't see them that way. And if you look at stand-up comedians as the ultimate in begging for love, as somebody standing onstage saying, "Love me . . ." I think women do it in more subtle ways—"Love me . . . or else."

Rosie Shuster

"**I** WAS a straight man's daughter," said Rosie Shuster as she picked at the top of a pizza during our preinterview meeting. She was torn about being profiled for a book. She has a fear of the media from having stood in the shadow of four famous humorists: her father, Frank Shuster, of the Canadian comedy team Wayne and Shuster; her uncle, Joey Shuster, cocreator of the original *Superman* comic strip; her former husband, Lorne Michaels, producer of "Saturday Night Live"; and her boyfriend, Dan Aykroyd, of "Saturday Night Live" and The Blues Brothers. Justifiably, Rosie was nervous that she'd be asked only about the men in her life. On the other hand, she has reached a point of new assurance in her career—she has found her voice and wants to set the record straight about who Rosie Shuster is and what her humor is all about.

Rosie gained her first professional experience writing facetious questions for a kiddie quiz show. She has written for "Saturday Night Live" since its inception, she has written for Lily Tomlin, "Laugh-In," and dozens of comedy shows in her native Toronto, Canada. Rosie's current projects include a television special based on the best-seller *Titters: The First Collection of Humor by Women* and a film, which she is writing with her partner, Wendy Apple.

–D.C.

Your father was a famous comedian in Canada. Were you encouraged to be funny as a child?

To get my parents' attention. There was a subtle pressure to be precocious, an emphasis on being cute and saying funny things.

Did you compete with your dad for laughs?

Not at that point. I thought everybody's parents were in the media because I used to listen to my father on the radio and that was natural to me. Only later did it seem weird to me that other people's fathers didn't do radio or television shows.

Did you think that your father was funny when you were a kid?

Yeah, I thought he was pretty funny sometimes. I thought he was pretty *corny* sometimes. You know there is a fine line between laughing and groaning.

What do you mean?

You know, puns and stuff. This is the first joke he ever taught me: He'd say, "We're having duck for supper," and I'd say, "Oh boy—duck!" And then he'd say, "I don't know if it's a girl duck or a boy duck." I was about three and a half at the time and he trained me so that whenever we had duck, we'd do the duck bit. Of course, it didn't come up often because we didn't have duck that often.

Do you think you were courted because you are a famous person's daughter?

I was pretty oblivious to that aspect of things, except when I skipped a grade and then I became creepy and out of touch with the other "popular" girls. I felt they had a lot of contempt for me (in fact, they probably didn't notice me particularly). One girl, who was very "sucky"—her last name was Finkelberg—used to come home from school with me and I knew that she wasn't my friend, but she would just sort of follow me home. Once she was upstairs and my dad had just come out of the can. She went in and when she came out, she was screaming that she wasn't going to take a bath for a week because she had just sat on the same toilet seat as Frank Shuster. I really wanted to vomit.

That made you angry.

Yeah, it pissed me off. I mean, it wouldn't be in my mind today if it didn't stick with me as some kind of: Oh, yeah—people can like you for fame by association.

How did you get together with Lorne Michaels?

One day on his way home from high school, Lorne spied me jumping wildly up and down on a pile of boards in an empty construction site, emitting little premenstrual whoops of joy. Soon he was walking me home, capturing my interest, telling me shocking firsthand accounts of teenage sexual practices going on in *my* high school. I was very sheltered. I ate it up. By fourteen I was going around with him and by twenty-two we were married.

Do you think you had an effect on Lorne's sense of humor?

I would imagine I did. It is harder to pin down now—I shy away from that question, I guess—but I remember in the early days of our being together, I was pretty shy and withdrawn and he was outspoken. Sometimes at parties I'd whisper lines in his ear, which he'd then repeat out loud and get a big laugh! When it drove me nuts that *he* got *my* laugh, he would say, "Well, then—say it yourself!" He wasn't trying to steal from me or anything, I was just so shy that he would be my guinea pig. I'd try out material through him. See, by the time I married Lorne he was also a straight man in a comedy team, just like my father. I was afraid to have a baby in those days because the doctor might say, "Congratulations! You have just given birth to a six-pound straight man!" And I'd scream, "Ahhh!" And that would be my life . . . and then I would die and my straight man would go on and have other straight men.

Did you work with Lorne professionally before he created "Saturday Night Live"?

He and I had worked together before SNL in Los Angeles and Toronto. I confess now I twisted his arm to get me a writing job on the Lily Tomlin Special because she was my idol. I was frothing at the mouth to have that job. I really applied all the pressure you read about women applying to their husbands or to men of great influence to give them jobs. I focused all the wrath and fury and frustration of a thousand denied Canada Council Grants on writing for Lily. Otherwise, I could have grown old in Toronto applying for grants and being a hack. I had no sophistication, no practical sense of how to deal with the bureaucracy. They were a gray, faceless mass with money in their pockets—and I couldn't even find the pocket. I would attach myself to people I thought were more financially shrewd than I was, pathetically hoping they would somehow help me. But I trusted that if I started with writing, which I was more or less secure about, I could start performing it, producing it, directing it, and then other things would naturally follow.

Are you encouraged by your peers at SNL when you write a good piece?

Sometimes. I bounce between feeling awkward about taking credit for things and feeling like I'm gypped and nobody knows which ideas were mine. So I'm either a mouse, too shy to say, "That's mine," or I'm an over-compensating, credit-hungry monster, tapping people on the shoulder till they say, "Shut up! We know you wrote that!" Another problem I had was overanalyzing things. I was censoring myself as I was writing and I couldn't even finish a sentence, let alone a page or a sketch or a movie. I kept seeing what was wrong with something before it was finished. I used to lead with my weak hand and then never follow through, so I never had any sense of having strength. I used to sneak monologues onto "Laugh-In," though. That was my first real TV writing experience.

How did you feel when you saw your material used on "Laugh-In" but couldn't take credit for it? Wasn't that frustrating?

No. Then it was a thrill that they'd do my stuff. I thought *I* had the last laugh. At that point in time I was just so green and desperate to hear something I had written Out There in the world that I thought it was a big private joke. They were doing *me* a favor.

Having come up in the shadow of famous men, is it difficult to project yourself with assurance?

Consistently with assurance? Yes. I need to go off by myself a lot. It *is* hard to do it in the shadow of a man because there's a temptation to fall back on the man and not produce yourself. If he's strong, he'll catch you. It's seductive to be weak.

Do you have a firm idea of who Rosie Shuster is?

It's getting much clearer all the time. Though there remains some confusion about my name. I was born Rosalind Shuster and Rosie was a nickname. I was called "Rosie Apple" when I was four years old by the bus driver who took me to nursery school. I called him "Glen Glen, the Big Fat Pen," which I thought was hysterical. I always liked the periods in my life in which I was called Rosie. After Lily's special, I wrote a shitty show that I didn't want on my resume and I used the pseudonym "Sue Denim." I've been Rosie Shuster, Rosie Michaels, Rosalind Shuster, Rosalind Michaels, Rosie Apple—and some part of me thinks that one wonderful game plan would be to write and do different projects under different names. You could keep up a subterfuge and not have everything traceable back to you.

How do you build up your confidence so you can back your work with more conviction?

I don't know. I'm going through a change again and I don't have any ready answers for that question, except that you have to admit to yourself that you want it first. I used to mix up fantasies and goals. I didn't have goals, I had only fantasies—and because I never made my fantasies my goals, I never went anywhere. Meanwhile, I couldn't help noticing that other people were achieving, you know?

If you were going to be remembered for one piece that you wrote for "Saturday Night," what would it be?

That's hard. I'm fond of Todd's seduction of Lisa in "The Nerds," which Anne [Beatts] and I created. I can't really respond to the question, I can just think of the last piece I worked on.

What was it about?

It was a mother-daughter sketch that Maureen Stapleton and Gilda did. It wasn't written for laughs, which was to me the departure from the usual slapstick. But there were laughs in it because of audience recognition of a classic situation. I was trying to capture the "Mother as Martyr" kind of thing that I'm trying to understand in my own life right now. I liked where the comedy came from because there were no jokes plotted at all, and that was the bravest thing about writing it. If there is one thing I accuse myself of and I try to watch out for, it is being facile. You can make an audience laugh if you think about it long enough and study it—a computer could probably write jokes. So in an age that is full of computers, you want to do something that a computer can't. I've never thought about that before—I'm thinking out loud now—but it is true. I'm fond of an ad parody I did for "A woman's product so personal even *we* don't know what it is." The package was a pink box with a black inverted triangle on it. It was an absurdly rude prop. The product itself was supposed to give a woman confidence. It was a useless and pointless product but women bought it because they are constantly becoming victims of Madison Avenue's assault on their self-confidence.

Do you find comedy writing a fulfilling job?

At times. It's a fine line between taking yourself seriously and not taking yourself too seriously. But you have to take yourself seriously enough to act, to do what you set out to do. If you don't take your work seriously, you will leave it unfinished. I'm in the process of moving now and I have millions of projects all over, crates of unfinished material. They're like bogeymen that are going to rise up out of the crates, waving their fingers at me. I get so depressed at the thought of moving all this shit around with me. I don't have furniture at this point in time, just cartons of unfinished projects—joke set-ups waiting for punch lines. Thousands of them.

Do you have a preference between collaborating and working alone?

I like both. I've enjoyed collaborating, especially in comedy. It's lonely writing by yourself. You feel like a loon, locked in your office, jacked up on caffeine, talking to yourself through the typewriter and giggling—and that's when it's *good*. You can really slip away. It's good to write alone sometimes, though. This last year I did not write alone enough. In bigger projects like writing films and stuff, I want to get into a position where I feel less needy of partners. I think that will be good, and then I can write anywhere. I can write on top of Mount Everest if I want. All I'd need is a pen and paper and strong legs. I would like the freedom to do that.

You often collaborate with Anne Beatts or Gilda Radner or one of the other women on the show. Is it as easy to collaborate with a man as with a woman?

Sometimes. It depends on the man. A good man is hard to find. Some of my best partners . . . have I answered your question? Sometimes the atmosphere in a writers' meeting at "Saturday Night" is like a bunch of young comedy bulls, pawing the ground and making each other laugh hysterically. The air is filled with testosterone. There are at least fourteen male writers and then Anne and me, and occasionally Gilda or Laraine Newman. If Anne and I had a funny title for a sketch, that would be enough from us, whereas one of the guys might jump up on the desk and start acting the scene out, playing all the parts. There were so few women writers that we really had to support one another, just to be heard, if nothing else.

Did you find that the guys would ignore or resist your ideas because they didn't get your jokes?

Oh sure. There was an impotence sketch that we thought was pretty funny. It was a man's worst nightmare of what would happen if he was suddenly impotent. His parents would rush to the bedside of their "failure," people would start pouring over, bringing him candy and flowers, the media would report it. . . . But the guys just couldn't relate to it. I guess there are times you just don't want sympathy. They'd say, "Make him older—that couldn't happen to a thirty-five-year-old. Make him forty-five."

Could you convince them that it *was* funny and should be run anyway?

No. But privately, it was pretty funny—just their reaction to the piece. I haven't worked out a lot of theory about this stuff, but there is something in comedy writing that has to do with flirting with taboos. You have to get real close to them and tickle them, especially on TV where it is almost a game of what you can and can't get on the air. Religion is even touchier than sex in a way. You can say "penis" but you can't say "Jesus." Forget writing about Jesus' penis.

SNL has enjoyed a reputation as a ground breaker in comedy. Did you feel influential as a part of that group?

I did and I do, but I also felt invisible in the middle of it. Most people don't read up to "Shuster" in the credits. Plus I was publicity-shy for so long. I was totally uptight when interviewers would ask, "How did you get your job?" I would clam up. I was afraid of blurting out, "On my back—fucking the producer!"

Were you afraid that people would think that you had been swept in on Lorne's coattails?

Sure. And they did. My most paranoid vision of my life is that my dad attracted Lorne (to me) and Lorne attracted Danny. This is rough on my identity.

Does that anger come into your humor?

I think anger and hostility find their way into my humor at one point or another. It gives me an aggressive edge and a somewhat perverse, dark side.

Does expressing your anger that way give you a sense of strength?

I've often felt that humor for me was like sending pins and needles out of the fog. I've kept myself foggy and ambiguous and vague—it's a form of hiding. I'd use humor to assert myself when people pushed me too far and I wanted to get them to back off.

Where else do you find material for comedy?

Everything is grist for the mill. Anywhere there is pretension there's humor. Tragic family melodrama later gets turned over and becomes wonderful material for comedy. The stuff that is oppressive and repressive and suppressive bubbles out when you finally get out from under. That is when hostility really gets turned into comedy and that's good stuff.

The "Saturday Night" schedule leaves you little time

to go outside—literally—to look for new material. **Do you find your comedy focus narrowing as you get further into the season?**

It is a little like being in an aquarium, you know? And we feed off one another to a certain extent. You start thinking that if you do a sketch about the prop man, it would be the funniest thing in the world. Everybody would *love* that in Wisconsin! You can lose touch.

Have you gotten any feminist reaction to your work on SNL?

Well, at the end of the third year I met Gloria Steinem. I wanted to have a garbage can lid up as a shield in case she was going to give me flak. But she was amazingly understanding and sort of cognizant of the situation. The most feminist flak I've gotten has been internal, from inside myself. I have censored myself. There are pieces that are outrageously funny that put women down, but they also caricature something that's true about women and those are the most problematic pieces. Comedy can't be propaganda. If you are poking fun at life, then you have to include women. There were a lot of lines set up that were important in the early '70s about feminism and what was righteous and what wasn't, but ultimately I found them personally repressive and restrictive in terms of how far I'd go in making fun of things. I had to burst through them and I was really apprehensive about getting a lot of critical feminist reaction, but I did not get that much. But then I live in a tiny world and I never give out my phone number, so maybe I just didn't get those calls at all and there are conclaves of hostile feminists after my ass.

Where do you see comedy heading, Rosie?

Over my dead body. But seriously, I don't know. I think that the real innovators are people like Richard Pryor, who is probably the most creative person in comedy today. I think humor is going to have more to do with surprises, like Andy Kaufman busing his audiences out for milk and cookies. Personally, I would like to perform comedy more, even though I'd be terrified. I'd do it as comedy therapy. I like to think that everything is therapy because it's good for me, you know? It's going to free me.

Penny Marshall

I MET Penny Marshall in her suite at the Sherry Netherland Hotel at 4:00 P.M.—just as she was finishing breakfast. Old friends stopped by to visit on this, the last day of her New York vacation, and none seemed surprised to find Penny in her bathrobe. She is, as she puts it, lazy, preferring to spend her free time doing nothing more taxing than sleeping, reading or talking.

Actually, there's not much free time in Penny's schedule, and she's not so lazy she doesn't work the nearly sixteen hours a day necessary to star as Laverne in television's popular situation comedy, "Laverne & Shirley." Penny plays opposite Cindy Williams, the cynical realist opposite the dreaming idealist. The role seems to be a natural for Penny—her deadpan delivery, sarcastic wit and jaded viewpoint make her as funny off the set as on.

Penny grew up in a "comedy family"—her brother Garry, with father, Tony, produced "The Odd Couple" and now, "Laverne & Shirley." And she was married to Rob Reiner, star of "All in the Family" and son of the zany comedian, Carl Reiner.

–K.B.

Do you feel that humor is a male-dominated field?

It is a male-dominated field because it's an aggressive field. It's not that the comedy people I know will beat you up. It's just that they're constantly pitching and "on." Sometimes, it's intimidating for girls who are hired as apprentice writers. What they have got to do is fight. It's not that you've got to have as much confidence as the men have because they don't even consider it confidence—they're just babbling and you have to babble back and pitch back without feeling, "Is this wrong?" or, "Will they think I'm no good if I say this?"

Do you have that necessary assurance?

I guess, but I hate fighting and I hate talking real loud. So I used to sit around while they "let the boys do it," and then I'd get in what I had to get in. When I was starting out I went to see The Committee. It was male-oriented, like most of the groups. The girl just played the wife unless she was really good. She could be really good, but she'd have to have the guts or the confidence to say, "No, we're doing this sketch" or, "I'm going to do this." I didn't feel like waging that war so I just went along my merry way and into television where there are a lot of women's comedies. That's why when people say, "Well, isn't it hard for a woman to do comedy?" I say, "No," because I think there are more women on television. Whether they're funny or not is something else, but at least they have a part.

Do you see any difference in the way women in comedy are changing, from "The Lucille Ball Show," for instance, to what you are trying to do in "Laverne & Shirley"?

I'm on the wrong show to answer that! I'm just trying to be funny. We started out with a show we didn't know what to do with, anyway. I thought it was going to be about these two girls who weren't satisfied, who were struggling to survive—and some of that has been kept.

But the show took a turn somewhere along the line. People love the two girls and they love when we do really crazy things—big, broad, physical stuff which *is* fun to do. We have different kinds of scripts. One is the serious theme, in which you're allowed to sit and talk to the other person. These supposedly are our meaningful shows. And we have the script that builds to the high comedy scene, which is where we'll fly or fall down or throw pies or whatever—you sometimes feel like a jerk doing it. Cindy and I get in these overalls we work in half the time because we crawl around the floor and we say, "We're fools. We're assholes, aren't we?" and then we start giggling. It is fun. It's a certain kind of humor which may not be sophisticated to some.

So there is a lot of emphasis on physical humor? Do you think that's unusual for women comedians?

I don't know. It makes us laugh and we're silly enough to do it. I found that except for women like Lucille Ball and Carol Burnett, the girl was the neat and clean person. Mary Tyler Moore didn't fall down too much. But every so often we do question it—"Are we guys?" We beat up cops. "Don't we have respect for anything?" And I guess we don't. "Is it funny? Okay, we'll do it!" Sometimes it is hard on the show as far as women are concerned. I mean, whoever has cramps that week is not the most pleasant person to be around. And when the writing staff arrives, you announce before the run-through, "I'm sorry, I've got cramps" and they go, "Ah, not again. She's going be pleasant to work with this week." But sometimes things don't work and you say, "This doesn't work here" and they say, "Is it that time?" and you say, "Fuck off, don't blame everything on that."

Do the women writers say that?

Yeah, they say, "Didn't you just have it?" We have women writers on our show but they're hard to find. Maybe they're just not loose enough—it is a haphazard business, you know, with lots of working late, and some people want a social life. That's Cindy's complaint too—"I can't date anymore. I'm exhausted. Where's my social life?" You don't have one. This is it, you do this. Once in a while you go to one of those fancy parties you have to go to and say hello to all the other tired actors, and then when it's hiatus time and you can go around and see people, you feel guilty because you're not working. "Wait, should I be working now?"

You seem to be able to survive it, though. You've been with the show so many years.

Well, sometimes it has its effect. We get tired and we get less involved with the scripts. When we have the energy, we fight. "No, no, this is the wrong line, it should be this," and we add things to the show. We used to do a *lot* of that stuff, but you can't possibly keep it up. When you do, it's there where you're allowed to play out some of your fantasies. Like one time Cindy and I were supposed to sing "Blue Moon" for a talent show episode and we changed it all around until finally we were monkeys on roller skates singing "Abadabadaba."

Is what's funny to you pretty much in keeping with what Laverne would find funny?

Sometimes. It used to be we were really in tune with what we were doing. But after a couple of years, in order to make a story work in television, you've got to make "the buy," and I can't always accept it.

What's the buy?

It's the premise of the story. You have to buy that your character would know this information or do this action. For example, on one show, I overhear two girls talking about Carmine, Shirley's boyfriend: "Oh, isn't he something, he's hot stuff." "Isn't he going with someone?" "Yeah, but she must be a real idiot." So I overhear this talk about my friend, and they had written that I go to Carmine and say, "How dare you cheat on Shirley?" I get mad at him and bring Shirley up and say, "Tell her!" He tells her and she turns around and says, "Carmine and I have this arrangement where we're both allowed to date other people." I couldn't make the buy. Of all people, *I* would know they had an arrangement—I fixed her up with the guy! I couldn't make the buy and we screamed all week. I said, "It makes no sense. I know this. You are asking me to act a complete show that I don't believe. There's nothing inside me."

You'd think two women living together would probably know every detail about each other's boyfriend.

Sure, but sometimes when guys are writing you run into a problem. They just don't understand how women would act and feel. I remember in one show they had written a speech in which I say, "Oh, I'm gonna have circles under my eyes." I added a line—"I'm gonna have to use a ton of Erase." They said, "What is Erase?" "It's this stuff you use when the rings show. It's not a big laugh, guys, it's just life. Trust me." "What is it? Will people know? Is it a brand name?" I said, "Leave it alone. It's not a big laugh, but I need to say it." Sometimes they don't know what you're talking about, they don't understand what goes on inside. Sometimes they write things and we say, "A girl would never do this." The last script we did this year, they wrote a typical male line. It was for the tag scene, the scene that comes at the end between the last commercials. The scene was that Shirley is writing in her diary, "Believe your friends"—that was the theme of the show—and I come in with a guy and try to sneak into the bedroom. They let us go that far, then Shirley always stops us. She says, "What are you doing?" I say, "He's the carpet repair man, he's going to check out the carpet in the bedroom." "There are no carpets in the bedroom." They wrote in the script that I say, "Well, he's the plumber. I just want to suck his cock. What do you care?" They left it in the script because they wanted to get the censor's note—"Would you please delete 'suck his cock.'" But I don't know, I don't care how good a girl-friend you are, I would never come in and say that line, in real life. Maybe people do, but I would never say it.

You might not say it in earnest, but as a joke?

Even in a joke, they didn't write what a girl would say. It was a problem even with my own husband. We did a movie for television that Rob and a friend wrote called *More Than Friends*. We "do it" for the first time and she's confused and keeps leaving him. The theme was that it was more important for him having sex in college for the first time than it was for her, mainly because he was in love with her and she wasn't really in love with him. They wanted her to be flippant after the sex scene and say, "When is the psych term paper due?" I said, "No, I don't think she feels that way, being brought up with the 1950s morality. The first time you do it you feel you're real dirt, you'll never get married. It doesn't matter whether you like him or not. I can't be in this other mood." They kept saying, "But it's not important to you." "He may not be important to me, but the act of doing it for the first time is." They just didn't understand.

Have you seen any improvement as more and more women are writing scripts?

With certain women. On our show it depends when they were growing up. It's all very confusing.

What were you like growing up? Were you always funny?

I asked that at my junior high school reunion after I found out that I didn't go with anybody. I was in love with everyone but I guess I never really went with anybody. I kept asking, "Did anyone go with me?" But I had a lot of friends, or I was desperately looking for friends. I'd always hang out with a group. I remember reading in my eighth grade diary—it was so pathetic— "Please make someone invite me to the Valentine dance" or, "Eddie hit me in the head with a snowball. I think I like him." I guess I kidded around. I would make fun of myself before anybody else could. I had braces and my hair in a ponytail—real attractive. And I came from a family where my mother would put me down. "That's what you're wearing? You look ugly!" So I would always hit before anyone could hit me. Self-defacing humor is my forte. I never really dreamed of being an actress, that was not my plan—I had no plan. But I was in dancing school because my mother taught dancing school. She used to drag us around to the USO shows and we were precision dancers, like the Rockettes, always ending with kicks. We did Fort Dix and Fort Hamilton. I never thought that was show business, I just thought that was my mother's quirk. On school nights she'd make us dance at the veterans' hospitals or insane asylums or Navy yards—as long as they'd feed us, we'd perform for food. "Will you feed these girls?" But I liked it mainly because the people stayed up late at night. That was my big lure to the business. They stay up at night wandering around, pacing at three in the morning. So I thought, "Ah ha, I'll stay up with these people."

And then you joined The Committee?

I wasn't in The Committee—I was too chicken—but I was in The Committee workshop. I idolized them 'cause they read newspapers. God, they were smart. They were the first group I saw when I went out to Los Angeles. But before L.A., I did a six-year stint in New Mexico—a whole other life. Married, baby, football player. I did a whole six years in New Mexico that has no relationship with my growing up or what I'm doing now. And I started doing a little theater there because those people stayed up at night and it was sort of fun. Then I came out to L.A. My brother was helpful: "Go take an acting class, get in a revue or something. Get temporary secretarial work 'till you can work out acting and unemployment. You won't work for ten years." I wasn't driven and I said, "Oh, okay, I guess this is what you do."

What attracted you to acting—besides staying up late?

I thought it was a heck of a way to make a living. I mean, I found out you could say only one word. I did "That Girl" and I had to say "Who?" That was my part. It was at the beginning of each show. It went, "There goes a girl with a head on her shoulders" and I went, "Who?" and they went "That girl." I said "Who" and got a hundred and twenty dollars. It was a pretty good deal—ten minutes' work I can make this, I don't have to do forty hours of typing. I thought that next time I could probably say "where" or "how." How about that? I can even say, "Who was that?" Seems pretty easy. And it was fun—you start hanging out with people who were in your classes.

What do you think that you, a comedienne, and your brother, a comedy writer, have in common?

We may disagree on a lot of things, but we do not disagree about what's funny. It's our attitude. We come from the same place.

What was that place like that could nurture two comedy kids?

Live up in the Bronx for twenty years—it's survival. You can either fight or you can laugh. When I first came out to L.A., Screen Gems was doing "The Flying Nun" and those kinds of series. I'd never work there. I wasn't an ingenue, I wasn't perky. I can't even fake it. My brother said, "It's because you've been through too much." If someone said, "Let's all get into the car and go down to the malt shop," everyone would be saying, "O-o-o-o" and I'd be saying, "How far is the car?" That's where I'm coming from. Maybe it's just laziness.

When you say something like that, "How far is the car?" are you aware that it's comical, it's a non sequitur?

No, that's just where I'm coming from, that's what I'm thinking about. Not what kind of ice cream I'm going to get, just how far my feet have to move to get there. Some people yell at me—"Oh, come on, you haven't seen daylight in four days." Well, is it far out there? But going back to my brother, I used to be embarrassed by the fact that he was a comedy writer. When I was in Albuquerque and he went out to Los Angeles and was writing for Jack Paar and Joey Bishop and the Dick Van Dyke Show and then was in a couple of them, my mother would call and say, "Garry is on the show." It would embarrass me, I don't know why. It was like *"My* brother?!" He didn't belong there. *We* didn't belong there. Even now, I still tend to feel, "What am I doing in Hollywood?" You also realize what is *anyone* doing in Hollywood? I mean, I go to an opening or a premiere—you're invited because you're a star—and I always look around for the stars. And it's just people I know and *we* are the stars! It's sort of funny to realize you're *it!* People are looking at you. But what is stardom? It's here and it's gone.

Do you feel more that you're just a woman who has a job, which is acting?

Well, I do feel like it's a job. Every so often I hate when I feel like it's a job but it does, unfortunately, get to that, because it just keeps going. But I only worked because it was fun. I never got into reading the trades every day and all of that. I still don't do that too much. I do go to the supermarket and see my face all over magazines. "Oh, what's happening in my life now?" They say "Laverne and Shirley split up." I say, "Oh, that one. Okay."

You seem to get bombarded with coverage in the movie magazines. Do you ever sue?

No. A couple of months ago they had me going with Ted Bessel.

Do you even know Ted?

Oh, yeah, I know Ted, he's a good friend. We went to dinner and someone took a picture. They had me "linked with handsome actor Ted Bessel—remember him from

'That Girl'?" I laughed and called Ted and said, "Guess what? We're linked." He said, "Oh, should we go to Mexico?" I said, "No, let's see what they do with it." But I found out that there's nothing you can do about it. In the fan magazines, if you try to sue them, it's a storefront, there's nobody there. Plus, that's what they do to exist. But I read the articles. At first I used to read everything. I couldn't believe my name was in print or why they would be talking about me, which I still can't quite figure out. And then I'd read about myself and say, "Oh, they got it all wrong. They got the wrong name. I didn't say that. They just didn't listen." Well, you find out that they're not true and they just make it up and there's not much you can do. But you also feel left out if they *don't* mention you.

But the people you would care about or work with would know that it's not accurate.

Yes, but it doesn't matter. I must say, myself, I'll pick up the *Enquirer* or something and it says, "They broke up," and I wonder if they broke up. You do get a slight seed of doubt.

What effect did being married to Rob Reiner, a comedy star and son of a famous comedy figure, have on you? Has he taught you things about comedy, or have you influenced him?

I don't think that kind of thing can be taught. I mean, you do something because that's the way you do it. I don't know how comedy is taught. There are certain rules of writing, I guess, but you can't give someone a sense of humor. You can tell them that supposedly things in threes can be funny, or words with *K* in them.

But if you're taking a script—just words on paper—how do you make it funny?

It's up to you and what you think is funny. I remember once being in an acting class and watching a girl do a scene. She was crying through the scene and I thought it had some of the funniest words I'd ever heard in my life, but this girl had tears running down her face. And then I actually read the words and I said, "This is a *funny* monologue." I don't know—maybe she was doing an exercise on how to cry. So I waited a respectable amount of time so people would forget she did the scene crying and I came in and got laughs. So anything can be played either way. It's the way you envision it. There are times when you're wrong. I could say, "This is funny," and it could fuck up the entire show. I'm told, "You must take this moment seriously," and I say okay. But I don't know how to give someone a sense of humor.

Do you try to find the humor in most situations?

You gotta or you'll die. I have to laugh at the ludicrousness of my life at times. I remember once I came home really upset. I was in a terrible mood and I'm whining—I'm a big whiner. Tears were running down my cheeks and my daughter came in an hour later than she should on a schoolnight and I'm trying to be mother, "What are you doing coming in late? You're grounded." Rob's staring at me and I went to the refrigerator to get some cheesecake that I brought home from the show the night before. I'm really upset and crying and Rob says, "Where did you get the cheesecake?" And I knew the line that was going to come out of my mouth was, "A man in a bunny suit gave it to Cindy and me." That's what happened—a man in a bunny suit came down to the show and gave us the cheesecake. I was so upset, but when I told him, we just laughed. I mean, how many people get to say that? It was just ridiculous and I said, "Okay, my life is a sketch, it's all a game." You know, that sort of sense of humor about things comes in handy. Next to sex my favorite thing is laughing—it's a part of sex. Make me laugh—I'll love you.

Have you tried to make people laugh so they'll love you?

No. I think if you make them happy, they'll like you. But when I'm meeting someone, I get scared trying to be "on." I'm not good at that kind of thing.

But when you're acting, does being "on" come easy? Is that ever a problem on the show, if you're in a bad mood, or the wrong mood?

Sure, sometimes there are problems. We get testy at times. We have a bad reputation—we're known as "The Cunts." Nice, huh? And it's because they're all a little frightened. I mean, here are two girls in a powerful position. I don't feel that powerful about it, but we know more about the show than anyone who is writing it because we've been there longer. And they're a little intimidated because they don't know how to talk to girls. It's like they're asking for a date. And also, when we get upset sometimes, we *do* cry, but there's nothing wrong with that—only men are afraid to cry—it's a relief. But sometimes they think they should handle us a certain way. Just talk, be a person.

You were talking about the physical humor of Carol Burnett and Lucille Ball earlier. Who have your role models been?

I wanted to be Doris Day, but I didn't have a shot at it. But I love Doris Day—she's so pretty. I guess men were role models more. I idolized men. I was taught they were gods. But then they disappoint you and the idols fall. You realize no one is an idol. I never thought of going into this business, but here I am.

Swoosie Kurtz

MY FIRST contact with Swoosie Kurtz was through her father, Col. Frank Kurtz, an animated and charming man, who would patiently take messages while Swoosie was out. When I met Swoosie in her New York apartment, it was clear that she had inherited her father's easygoing, friendly manner. She had just returned to New York from California after the cancellation of the short-lived "Mary Show," with Mary Tyler Moore, and she was delighted to be back home.

Swoosie is a classically trained actress with contemporary sensibilities and a sense of humor that can be childlike or downright bawdy—a combination that has yielded critical praise and awards. For her role in *Uncommon Women and Others*, Swoosie was honored twice: once with a Drama Desk Award nomination and once with an Obie Award for best actress. Her performance in *Tartuffe* earned her a Tony nomination for best actress. And in 1977, the Drama Desk Award for best actress in a musical was bestowed on Swoosie for her outstanding performance in *A History of the American Film*.

—D.C.

That's a very unusual name, Swoosie. How did you come by it?

I was named after a B-17 my father flew in World War II. It was called "The Swoose." It was a combination of old parts and new parts. My mother was going to name me Margo after her, but the plane was famous, my father was famous (the press was always writing him up—he was the most decorated pilot in the war and he was the only man to be on three Olympic diving teams). . . . So when I came on the scene the press wrote, "The other Swoose has landed." The nurse put it on the birth certificate and there it stood. My parents felt, well, okay, everybody seems to have latched on to it and liked it. I love it now. In this business people probably think I made it up for the stage or something, but who could make that up?

The name sounds like a cross between a swan and a goose—kind of humor-oriented in itself.

It's interesting to get people's reactions to it before they meet me or before they've seen me act. They have a picture of a "Swoosie" in their head and when they meet me they say, "Swoozie! I expected a blonde with big tits!" Everybody tends to pronounce it Swoozie, with a z. But I don't mind because everybody does it. It makes me think of floozy and that whole image. People have said to me, "Aren't you worried about that name? I mean, can you see Swoosie Kurtz playing Hedda Gabler?" Of course I can. In fact, I *did* Hedda Gabler.

I can't quite place your accent. Where did you grow up?

I was born in Omaha, but I grew up all over because my father was in the Air Force.

So you were an army brat?

Yeah, exactly. I went to seventeen schools before high school. Then I went to USC on scholarship for two years. I gave it up to go to London to study at LAMDA (London

Academy of Music and Dramatic Art). Then I came to New York, and I've been here ever since.

What was your first acting job?

I was in a water show when I was about three years old in Miami, Florida, at the Deauville, that big, gorgeous hotel. My father was diving or something. It wasn't a commercial show that you paid to see; it was just a thing that was going on that night. They let me do a little water act. I did the backstroke. Of course, I was about three feet tall and weighed about forty-two pounds, and I used to click around the pool in little gold lamé slippers. A lady said to my mother, "There goes a little Sarah Bernhardt." So I was doing the water show—it was at night, very dramatic, spotlights on me—doing the backstroke. I would finish and be about to begin the breaststroke, but first I would go over to the side of the pool and get my towel. I would delicately dab my eyes, then start into the water again. But they took the spotlight off me and began the next act! I said, "Hey! Wait a minute! I'm not finished! I'm not finished!" This little three-year-old! So I think that ever since then I've been trying to get that spotlight back. I was in a production of *The Drunkard* ("Father, dear father, come home with me now. . . .") on an air base somewhere, an entirely forgettable performance, I'm sure. I wanted to be a ballerina when I was eight years old, and I read a book about Pavlova. I read that she was a perfectionist and was the greatest prima ballerina in the world at that time. But Diaghilev told her that she had a little fault with her right toe, she was a little off-center. To be absolutely perfect, it should have been adjusted one degree. Diaghilev said, "Forget about it, Anna. You're the greatest ballerina in the world." "No, no," she said, "I must work on this. Will you help me?" So she worked for five years every day to correct this tiny flaw. I was just knocked out. I finished the book on a Friday night and declared that by Monday morning I was going to learn how to do a split. All weekend I stretched and stretched. I didn't succeed. I still can't do a split. The point is that at eight years old I was so inspired by this biography I set myself that deadline. It reminded me much later of Rita in *Uncommon Women and Others*, saying, "Boy, when I'm thirty I'm going to be pretty fucking amazing. . . ." "When I'm thirty-five I'm going to be pretty fucking incredible. . . ." And then at forty-five she says the same thing. She keeps putting it off. That's what I'm still doing in real life. I said I was going to be in a Broadway musical by the time I was thirty, and I wasn't—but I was thirty-three. I say now that I'm going to star in a real Broadway musical by the time I'm thirty-five. Well, that's this year.

What was the musical you did?

Christopher Durang's *A History of the American Film*, in the spring of 1979 on Broadway. It was real neat.

What kind of part did you play?

The character was called "Bette," a Bette Davis type. The show was based on movies from the 1920s to the '70s. It started with the silents. It was total satire time, completely off the wall. We went through all the genres: the westerns, the I'll-Cry-Tomorrow movies, the early gangster movies, '50s musicals, Busby Berkeley-type movies. I played Dr. Strangelove, among other parts.

Maintaining the Bette character the whole time?

Yes. There were main parts. The lead was a Jimmy Cagney character, tough little guy who gets all the women. Then the second character was the ingenue, the one with blonde hair, playing a sort of Lillian Gish in the silents. Slowly she became an alcoholic and was given polio in one movie because she had to go through something. She had to suffer. She turned out to be Elizabeth Taylor in *Virginia Woolf*. I was the third in this triangle—the other woman, the bitch goddess—Bette Davis in a speakeasy who's mad about a guy and he won't give her the time of day. It was a wonderful, mad piece of humor. I was Joan Crawford, Betty Grable and an Andrew sister all within the same character. The writer got us all to Hollywood so we were in the movies during the '30s and '40s. It was amazing how Durang strung these characters through all these years and yet they remained the same people. One of the leads played Ma Joad in *The Grapes of Wrath* and went offstage and came back as the Virgin Mary, ran offstage and came back as a Busby Berkeley show girl in a number called "We're in the Salad." Instead of "We're in the money," it was, "We're in the salad, we're in the salad, we got a lot of what it takes to fill a bowl." There were six of us in that number. There were supposed to be one hundred show girls—and there were six of us.

Is Bette Davis someone you identify with as an actress?
Yes.

To me, she's a very funny actress.
Yes. She has that incredible range, which I think Rosalind Russell also had, although she was a more overt comedienne. But they could each take a real situation and make it funny without doing any kind of *shtick*. Their slant on things, their view of something. . . . Bette Davis was one of my idols, she was so rounded, had such range. She was not one of those stars who always played herself.

Is it difficult for you to play Swoosie Kurtz?
Yes. It's terrifying. That was one of the problems with the character in "The Mary Show."

Why do you think that show failed?
It wasn't any good. We did *some* good stuff. We taped eleven shows and three were shown. Through some miracle of bad taste, they chose the worst stuff we had done.

What kinds of problems do you run into working for TV, given that you're a perfectionist and trained to work for the stage?

In some ways, of course, after you've worked on the stage, TV is like falling off a log. You don't have to deliver. Onstage you have to deliver, with no help, eight times a week. People can say you're wonderful and come backstage and regale you one night. You go home and you feel terrific and the next day you wake up and have to go through it all again for people who haven't seen it. In television the acting is almost the least important part. For instance, we were rehearsing a sketch for "The Mary Show" and Jim Hampton had a line right after mine. The director said to him, "Oh, Jim, don't come in too quickly with that line because Swoosie's gonna get a laugh on that." I thought, "Must be my inimitable delivery!" But I was curious as to how he knew. I said, "That's lovely, but how do you know?" He said, "Oh, we'll put one in." We were going to do it in front of a live audience, and presumably the whole reason for the live audience is to get live human beings laughing in their own timbre and rhythm. Well, not so. They overkill it with that goddamn laugh track. I saw the show I just spoke of, and for me, that alone killed it. What happens is that they're so panic-stricken in television, they work out of fear, totally. The axe always hangs right above your head. I was praying that "The Mary Show" would be over because I didn't want to sign a contract in the first place. Everybody else was praying that they could support their wives and kids, their husbands, which I don't have. I'm mobile, so I don't care. I could go back to New York within a week and be delighted. But everyone else was saying, "Oh God, we gotta make this good, we gotta." You can't work like that. The key word in television is dilution. That's what happens to your work, it gets diluted. To continue what I was saying before, they put in the laugh track so that it covers the punch line! Human beings cannot laugh that quickly, that intently. It's like a machine gun. It's so unnatural. I watched a sitcom the other night, Stockard

Channing in "Just Friends," because I think she's incredibly talented and I wanted to see what they could do with somebody like that on TV. I have been offered my own series. Maybe it could just work under the right circumstances. So I figure this show is a good test. If they can let her do good work, then maybe it could work for me too. But there was that damn laugh track again. Once again, they just can't trust that the guy at home is going to sit and laugh by himself. The laugh track may be necessary, but they should learn to use it in a way that doesn't interfere with the action on the screen. One of the first rules in comedy—when you're not getting a laugh—is, can the audience hear the line? If they can't, of course you're not going to get a laugh. Maybe you're turning upstage at the moment, or somebody may be moving over here and they're aurally just missing it. I think that in TV they cover up a lot of good work that way. To me, that's a lot of what happened to "The Mary Show."

You seem to have had no trouble in developing your personal acting style in humor.

I think that's an innate thing, a sense of rhythm and timing, and thank God I have it. You really can't be taught that. I'm a great imitator, which is basically what all acting is and is also a vital ingredient in humor. And I don't mean in a cheap sense of imitation either. I did *The Effect of Gamma Rays on Man-in-the-Moon Marigolds* for many years, and one of the mothers we had was Carolyn Coates, a wonderful actress, and I started doing certain consonants and vowels just like she did.

Do you steal material?

Yeah, I do. When I see good acting I steal everything I can get, absolutely everything. I ran into Mary Beth Hurt out in L.A.; she was doing a play and I went backstage to see her and she greeted me with, "Swoosie! I imitate you in this play—something you did in *Uncommon Women* that I stole from you." I was so pleased and I said, "My God, that's the highest form of flattery!" The funny part is that I stole the same gesture from an actress in *Vanities*, then Mary Beth stole it from me. She *thought* she had stolen it from me but when she did it, she made it her own. When I had stolen it, I had made it my own.

Do you have a preference in performance? Do you prefer doing drama or humor, or is it just the role that wins you over?

Just the role. Just a good play.

Is there a part that you would like to play that you haven't yet?

Regan in *King Lear*, Sabina in *Skin of Our Teeth*. I'd like to do a musical. I also love plays about the rich—Philip Barry, *The Philadelphia Story* and *Holiday*—because they're great escape. I'm not rich, but I think people love to see stories about the rich, as they did during the Depression.

Do you fantasize to flesh out a role?

Definitely. I think that's how my imagination got developed as a child—not having brothers or sisters, being alone and having to entertain myself. Lots of times I'd do my homework on the road when we'd be traveling for a month and my folks couldn't put me in school. I would have to do it on my own, set my own deadlines, say that now I will do a hundred pages of this math over the next three weeks. I was my own little teacher.

Is there anything you do, an exercise, say, when you're working out the kinks on a particularly difficult part?

You mean like working on a part in rehearsal?

Trying to get hold of a character before performing it.

Yes. I have a whole series of things I go through, most of which I learned at LAMDA. They gave us a methodical way of analyzing first a play and then the part. I work a lot from the outside in. I can't just artificially dig down for the emotions and dredge them up, have them spew out. That's one way of working but it's not my way. If I can get a walk down or picture the character: Whether this character wears a hat; whether she picks her nose; whether she slouches or stands up straight; then I'm on my way. The ball starts rolling and I say, "Ah ha! She slouches!" Well, that means that maybe she doesn't think too much of herself or maybe she was too tall at age thirteen, so she had to slouch. Habits too: does she smoke? doesn't she smoke? None of these may come across onstage. Obviously, if it's in the script that she doesn't smoke I'm not going to light up and impose that on the play, but it's important to think, does this person have physical ills? Does she prefer it hot or cold? What are her weaknesses? Where does her tension go? Does she get headaches? I'm getting too detailed; more generally a character is really rich and I like to search for that depth. What that exercise does is, it starts me asking a lot of questions which then lead to other tangents. When I started working on *Tartuffe* with John Wood, I thought I was stuck with a boring, stilted ingenue. I thought it would be a straight part and I had no idea in the world how I was going to do it. Straight is boring to me.

By "straight" do you mean reading the script and interpreting it in a limited or literal way?

Yeah. Those little girls who come in and say, "Oh, yes, father, whatever you say, father" just bore the shit out of me. I had been playing all these wild characters—neurotic and expressive ladies—and suddenly I was stuck with what I thought was a real clinker. So I sat here, on this very sofa, and I went through the play—everything the character said, trying to figure out how I could bend it a little, how I could slant it, asking how is she off center? Everything she did I made excessive, extreme. I think that speech patterns are important for a character—the words one chooses to use. You'll notice if you go through a play carefully that a character will tend to repeat certain words, certain phrases. For instance, she is constantly saying, "Yes, father, yes, father." You could look at that and think, "Oh, isn't that boring; it's just another 'Yes, father.'" But I thought, "If she's saying, 'Yes, father,' what is she thinking inside? She's probably an incipient hooker." Take a wild example: all the time she's sitting there saying that she doesn't mean it at all. She's saying, "Yes, father," but in her head she's thinking, "But I'm going to go ahead and do what I want to." So on opening night, a very famous man, who shall remain nameless, came up to me and said: "You must know music, because what you did in that scene was amazing, it was pure music." It was just another dumb line, another "Yes, father," but because of the way I unconsciously orchestrated it, it came out hilarious. It got one of the biggest laughs in the show.

What do you do if you interpret a character differently, let's say, from the way the director does? How do you win that person over so you can play the character the way you feel will work?

That's tricky. You have to give him, the director, chapter and verse as to why the character would behave this way as opposed to the way he sees it. Sometimes you're both talking about the same thing, but you're saying it differently. He's saying, "She has to get angry here." You say, "No. I don't feel she is. I feel that she's hurt by what he has just said." Most likely the director is giving you a result. He wants to see the reaction, which is anger. What you're saying as an actor is, "No, no, what he just said hurt me. It's possible that I'll get angry because of that, but right now in the process of rehearsal, I can't show you anger because I have to go through the other phase first, which is letting him say that to me, absorbing it, getting my reaction to it and then maybe out of defense, I'll get angry at him."

Do you think it's more difficult to get an audience to laugh or to cry?

To laugh.

Why?

For one thing, because Lord Olivier said so and he's no slouch! He said that after performing the greatest comedies and the greatest tragedies, it's much easier to make people cry. I think so too. Laughter is much more complex somehow. I have often been in previews of a play and I will get upset because certain scenes are not getting laughs. I would talk to my friends after the show and say, "What's the matter with that scene? They're not laughing!" They'd say, "Swoosie—that's a very touching scene. We don't want to laugh at that." In *Ah, Wilderness!* when I get my first kiss, the scene is filled with laughs and yet at a certain point it becomes nostalgic for the audience because they remember *their* first kiss. They don't laugh because they are moved. So sometimes actors will become obsessed with laughs when they should trust the text (if it's a good play) and say, "Okay, maybe they're just listening at this point and that's why they're not laughing." We've all heard of cheap laughs. Well, I think there's such a thing as a cheap cry. It's pretty easy to jerk a tear out of somebody. It's much more tricky to get people to laugh.

In many ways it's a much more personal reaction.

Yes, it is. It's very personal. To get people to laugh for the right reason, too, is very difficult.

You seem like you'd be a great film actress. Are you going to do more of them?

Well, that's what some people say about me and I just hope that the right people think it. And pretty soon. I've done a few films but never a big part. I did *Slapshot* with Paul Newman and I played a very funny part, a hockey wife with hair teased out to here—the old sprayed-on helmet look. George Roy Hill, the director and a wonderfully funny man, came up to me during the scene I was doing and said, attempting to pat my head, "Darling, this is what we want here. . . ." and he literally got his finger caught in my hair and couldn't get it out! I wore pointed tits and chewed gum. I started out with two lines and they were nothing. The first day on the set I did one line and George said, "Swoosie, we're going to write you into a few more scenes, okay?" They loved what I was doing—whatever it was.

Were you allowed to improvise?

Not really for the dialogue, but I did expand on my reactions. In one scene in *Slapshot*, three of us hockey wives were sitting in the stands (the other two were my shadows; they didn't say too much and always sat on either side of me). I had on an imitation leopard coat—terrible, terrible wardrobe—and one of the wives said something like, "You know, I think I'm going to get Lou one of those games about life where you learn history and architecture." She went on and on about how she was going to try to educate her husband and I said, "Yeah. You can only drink and screw so much of the time." They were having this massive slaughter on the ice, blood all over the place, and people are saying, "Youmother-fuckingcocksucker. . . ." The fans get bloodthirsty and shout these horrible things and I look around and say, "Good crowd."

Then I played the wife of Ryan O'Neal's best friend in *Oliver's Story*. I also did a film called *First Love*, which was a real bomb-arooni. I did a nice scene in that film with Bill Katt, but it was cut. It was nice anyway; I got flown to Oregon.

Have you ever been allowed to write in lines in plays?

Yeah. I have occasionally written a line or three in plays that I've been in. Obviously not Molière, but in something like *Uncommon Women* I was responsible for a couple of the lines. I want to tell you something about *Uncommon Women*, which I just thought of. It has to do with getting people to laugh for the right reasons. The character of Rita in that——you saw it on TV, right? Well, you didn't see the version with the raucous language because we couldn't do that on public television, believe it or not. I had a speech about cocks, that our entire society is based on cocks—buildings, roads, shopping malls. Of course on TV it became that society is based on the *phallic* principle, which is not at all the same as cocks. On TV you can say anything clinical about the body but you cannot say anything about the body in the vernacular. You can say "penis" but you can't say "cock." Well, to me "penis" is a much more offensive word than "cock." "Cock" is a nice healthy upfront kind of word. "Orgasm" was fine. I could say that. Couldn't say "hell." I was appalled! What is public television for? You can't say "bastard" or "bitch." Every night I hear them say it on NBC, CBS—it's so dumb. One of my most shocking lines in the play referred to women's liberation and freedom. The line is, "I've tasted my menstrual blood!" Well, I knew that if I pulled back or seemed grossed out by that line, the audience would sense it and pull back too. I had to fully commit myself to the line and hope for the best (naturally, I hoped for a laugh). Happily, my theory was proved right in previews of the play. I would come out fully committed, deliver the line and there would be a moment when the audience would think, "Did you hear what she said?" and then they'd laugh. That's what I mean by getting people to laugh for the right reasons. It has to be done with taste, even the most tasteless things, which that part could be if played by the wrong actor.

Do you consider yourself a feminist?

A lot of that has to do with a certain kind of honesty I feel women are sharing more and more. I grew up somewhat suspicious of friendships with women because in school I could relate better to men. Somehow, the girls seemed to have slightly ulterior motives about things. When a boy said something to me, I felt he was saying exactly what he meant—nothing more, nothing less.

Whereas with a girl, I wasn't sure if she was being entirely straight with me. I found that as I grew up, my lasting friendships were with men. Since doing *Uncommon Women*, however, I have changed my mind about women. I find now that I value my women friends more than ever, and I find women so *reliable*, so deeply dependable. I'm sorry that for all those years I felt a kind of suspicion around them. I think women are being more honest and open about things now and as a result, they are coming out as fuller human beings. Somebody said to me before I went to L.A. to do "The Mary Show": "I just want to say one thing to you before you go out to do that show. You're going to be doing sketch material, you're going to be clowning around, you're going to be funny. Don't lose your sexiness." I thought, how odd! But that's a good point. It used to be that a woman would have to lose her femininity to be funny, like Lucille Ball or Carol Burnett. They're real clowns and they became neuter in a way. Hopefully, we can be funny now without losing our sexiness or our femininity. It doesn't mean that we have to be dainty and cautious, or hold back. Men are accepting that more, I think. When my agent came to see *Uncommon Women*—nine women in the cast, no men—he came up to me and said, "Well, Swoosie, you were wonderful, everybody's work was wonderful, but of course I can't relate to the play because it's all about women." Three of us were standing there and we all jumped on him. "Listen, in school we had to read *Moby Dick, Lord of the Flies, Catcher in the Rye*. Did we say, 'We can't relate to this book because it's all about a guy?'" Do we watch a movie like *The Graduate* and say, "Oh, that's about a man, so I enjoy watching it but I can't relate to it." It's just ridiculous! You relate to *people*, not to men or women. But strangely enough, he wasn't the only person who said that. People would say, "What do I know about five women at Mt. Holyoke College?" I wanted to say, "Well, watch and learn."

What kind of chances do you think other women humorists have for success and recognition?

I think better and better. I saw Monteith and Rand the other night, and she's wonderful. They're both wonderful, but she especially stands out. I think the world is much more ready for a kind of lady who can play a gig on the Carson show or Vegas or Tahoe and not be the second person on the bill, but rather the star act. But it's a handful, that's all.

What will you work on next?

I want to expand. Films are my next goal. I've decided that I would like to bypass television. I've just come to that conclusion in the past few weeks. The time I spent out in California was valuable in that it taught me what I *don't* want to do. Sometimes you've got to have that kind of measuring stick. I never wanted to do a series. They had to talk me into doing "The Mary Show." I turned it down over and over and the network kept coming back to me with an offer of more money and less time spent in L.A. So finally I figured I couldn't turn it down. I'm not at all sorry I did because it was terrific for me. I got nothing but good things from it, even though the show itself failed. I would love to do a film. I really would. Who wouldn't?

Gail Parent

GAIL Parent was one of the first female comedy writers in television. That was fifteen years ago and the list of credits she has accrued in that time confirms her position as one of the most successful comedy writers around, regardless of gender. She wrote the novel and, later, the screenplay (with frequent partner Kenny Solms) of *Sheila Levine Is Dead and Living in New York,* a second novel, *David Meyer Is a Mother,* the screenplay (with Andrew Smith) of *The Main Event,* plus numerous television specials and the cream of the variety shows—"The Carol Burnett Show," where she collaborated with Kenny Solms, "The Mary Tyler Moore Show," "Mary Hartman, Mary Hartman," which she helped to originate and the short-lived but highly regarded "3 Girls 3," which she also originated with Kenny.

–K.B.

When did you start writing comedy?

By the time I got to college, when I knew I had a sense of humor, but you couldn't major in humor. I didn't really

199

know there was such a job as comedy writing, that you could grow up and become a comedy writer. It didn't make any sense at that time. I was in the drama department and that's where I met Kenny Solms.

Were you writing or acting in the drama department?

I was actually wasting time and Kenny was going to be an actor. But the first big thing we did were some comedy albums, and Joe Hamilton, Carol Burnett's husband, heard one of the records. We had an interview with him and we were hired and brought out to California to write for "The Carol Burnett Show." We had a contract for seven weeks and I told my mother that I would be back very soon. Except for frequent visits, I never got back. I was married by the time I started writing. I thought it would be a good way to stay home and make a living.

What was your experience working on the Burnett show?

It was a great experience because it offered a lot of security. You had a weekly job which went on only half a year because they do reruns the other half, so we had a chance to do other things at the same time. During that period I wrote *Sheila Levine,* and we did a lot of specials— for Ann-Margret, Bing Crosby, Don Rickles. We did some situation comedies, one "Mary Tyler Moore Show," and later I also did "Mary Hartman" and last year we did a Broadway show, *Lorelei.* Some people work on variety shows and enjoy staying in variety. I always wanted to cover the media.

Have you covered all aspects yet?

Well, I've done magazines, books, plays, films, records. No radio yet.

Is Kenny still your partner?

For the last few years we had sort of an open marriage. We're not married to each other really, but I was doing other things and so was he.

What are the problems and advantages of working with a male collaborator?

Well, when Kenny and I first started out, before women's liberation, we were in our young twenties so it didn't look as if you could trust us to begin with and it was freaky to have a female comedy person. Kenny was also very aggressive—you know, the male counterpart in the team—and what we did together, I would never have had the nerve to do alone. That male/female aspect is valuable, and overlapped into our private lives. I was married, but I was the woman in Kenny's life for a long time, just working with him and being there. It was always interesting to bounce off of that. The good part about it is that neither one of us was afraid to work alone, so I could make my mark writing a couple of books and doing some television alone and know that I could do it, and the same with him. We wanted to be together rather than feeling we had to be together.

Initially, were there any problems working with him because of a difference in vocabulary or point of view? Or did any differences broaden your scope?

Again, it's like a marriage. If you go into it young enough, when you don't have your own habits, then you find you're thinking alike. And we found we were thinking very much alike. There was an ESP thing between us. I didn't have any problems with Kenny. There would be different points of view, but that's what you need.

You could work some of each viewpoint into what you were writing?

Well, no, what would happen is that you trust each other. If I said, "A woman would never say this," he would believe it. There's not so much of a distinction now, anyway—women say anything and men say anything and we're closer than we've ever been as male and female. But I think it was based on trust and instinct, not so much on male and female. A little more male and female went into *The Main Event*. It has a lot to do with men and women fighting and I really did a lot of fighting with Andrew Smith.

And you used that?

Yes. It's funny, I couldn't begin to collaborate with somebody I wasn't in sync with. It would be easier for me to spend a week with somebody I didn't know well and adjust to it than it would be for me to write with somebody I wasn't in sync with. So I don't really do it often, or find many people I could do it with.

Have you noticed any changes in the way funny women have been presented in television and the movies during your years in the field?

There have been stereotyped women in movies and television, but that was because women didn't write them. You're writing about yourself and if you really knew how a woman behaved, you wouldn't write a dumb, stupid, stereotyped role. The men were writing the stereotypes because they weren't writing from experience. I don't know what it's like inside a dumb blonde. I would probably be closer to a male character than the stereotype of a dumb blonde.

Are there fewer stereotypes as more and more women are writing?

Yes. What happened was that when "The Mary Tyler Moore Show" started, Jim Brooks and Alan Barnes started to employ women. Joe Hamilton did with me. He realized with Carol that it was a good idea. For several years I was the only woman writer. There were a lot of variety shows on, so there may have been seventy writers in the business, and I was the only woman.

Did the others turn to you for the feminine opinion—"Is this believable? Would a woman do this?"

It's an undercurrent, it's not that pronounced. On "The

Mary Tyler Moore Show," they started to realize that women went through experiences they could use, and that it was valuable to have female writers. However, the moment I say that women write better for women, I'm also saying that men write better for men. That's the unsaid version, which is not true. A good writer should be able to go through the experiences of either sex and get to know them. *David Meyer* is written in the first person male and I'm not saying that it's good or bad, but there is some accuracy in it.

What prompted you to write *David Meyer*? Was it a challenge to see if you could pull off a believable male character?

No, I don't think that any of this is premeditated. You get a feeling of what you can write or tell funny. I think it's wrong to believe you're going to start out to prove something. Or, the worse thing to say is you're going to do a commercial project—those usually aren't. You have to go on instinct or what you think is a funny story, what you think you can handle.

Carol Burnett is one of the first woman comedians to act out characters. Did you originate any of them when you were writing for the show?

We did a character that kept saying "George" in an annoying voice, we did a lot of movie takeoffs, we did Lucy Baines Johnson and Miss America and we created Marian on "As the Stomach Turns," the takeoff on soap operas.

Did you want to poke fun at certain qualities in these women?

It's not specifically the person. It's like doing a cartoon, you would exaggerate certain physical elements and certain mannerisms. It's mainly done out of affection. They were not devastating put-downs of the women.

With such a wide range of characters, it seems you must have found inspiration from the newspapers, tele-

vision, movies, or maybe from being in a supermarket and noticing a woman saying "George" in that special way.

You're absolutely right. It does come from what's happening in your environment. As a matter of fact, I find that it is hard for me to write a book on top of another book because they empty out all the ideas I currently have and I almost have to have some more life experiences to fill up again. People always accuse me—— I'll be in a room when something happens and they'll say, "Oh, you're going to write about that, right?" People think you're not living at the moment, you're filing. You know, it's like being with a psychiatrist, you think that he's analyzing you, that you're not just having dinner, but he's wondering why you're ordering shrimp cocktail.

And a comedy writer?

I have a lot of friends who also write comedy and it's funny because when I'm with them sometimes we say, "All right, who has custody of this conversation?" If you're talking about something funny that you've also written about, you have to declare that you have written about it and you are not just making conversation.

What was your inspiration for _Sheila Levine_? Your life at that point was just the opposite—you had graduated from school and gotten married, and Sheila was going to kill herself because she wasn't married.

It was really a projection of what I would have gone through. Since I had that marriage-oriented conditioning, some of it was imagination. Some of it was based on a close girl friend's experience. And now this friend says, "Next time you call and ask what's new, forget it!"

Was that your mother in the book?

Close to my mother, yes. My mother was Miss Atlantic City and the mother in the book is Miss Coney Island. See how cleverly I disguised her? My mother is much more aware, more loving than Sheila's mother.

Were you encouraged to be funny when you were growing up?

That's a good one, because I always thought that it was a real detriment. For one thing, you couldn't be serious. Once in college somebody gave me one perfect rose, which should have been a romantic moment, but I said, "Where are the other eleven?" Which is not funny but I was trying to be funny rather than go with the romance of the moment. Big mouth.

Because you were embarrassed?

Because I was embarrassed and that was my way of dealing with it. Definitely. I knew you could make friends by being funny. But there are a lot of women who are funny——it's a whole new era of women being funny and *feminine*, however. In my new life—I've been separated for a year and a half now—it's a first for me going out with and relating with men. I'm not finding a career and having to *prove* I'm funny, so I can actually go to dinner and not push it. If it were ten years ago, I would still have been trying to prove I was hilarious. Now I can save it for my work. Also, comedy can be aggressive and devastating and you can be afraid to be with somebody who is comedic, who uses that quick wit to put you down. But I've had a lot of experience with humor. I grew up with two sisters and the three of us all have good senses of humor. My mother and father too.

Some people who now have careers in comedy say they were real lonely as kids and that gave them the chance to be the observer and see that the emperor wasn't wearing any clothes. You, on the other hand, seem to have been surrounded by people who enjoyed life and enjoyed laughing.

I had a tremendous amount of security at home. There were never any shaky times. My parents were secure with each other, and my father was secure with work (he was a Wall Street executive). But my mother had this little bit of show business background, having been Miss Atlantic City and on the RKO circuit and a show girl. There are a lot of women who are funny, however, and not all of them use it to earn a living, as I did.

And some of them only show it when they're with other women.

I don't know, I don't think you can help it or control it. I'm not funny in an aggressive way, but I do appreciate a really good funny situation, whether it's with a man or a woman. In a one-to-one relationship with a funny woman, I think that men like to laugh and they like a woman to have a sense of humor. But it's not pleasant to be with somebody, either male or female, when they use the person they are with as the brunt of a joke. I don't have to control that because I don't really have it in me. I have more of a desire to, you know, feed a man food than I do to have one-up on him. Also, some people can't be with a man who isn't political, or doesn't have a certain look or whatever. The bottom line for me is a sense of humor. I cannot be with somebody who doesn't have one and it's got to be pretty sharp because I am surrounded all day by people who have tuned theirs carefully through experience, just by using it over and over. It's their whole means of making a living. So I do need somebody who makes me laugh and I've been lucky to have found some men who can.

What sort of things make you laugh?

First of all, the worst thing to do is to see a comedian or a film with comedy writers because they don't laugh a lot. They say, "That's funny," but spontaneous laughter is hard to get.

Because they're analyzing what's happening?

I think so. It's easy, though, to laugh at a situation. I laugh a lot. I get hysterical, but at what happens in real life rather than something that's been planned to make me laugh.

You were just saying that comedy writers are able to tune their sense of humor, to hone it to a sharp skill. How do you do that? How do you learn to be a good comedy writer?

You need a sense of humor and I don't know how you get that. From that point on, there really is some form to it. If you want to write situation comedy you have to know that a script is between thirty-eight and forty-two pages long, double-spaced dialogue. If you really watch it, you'll see that it's a problem of the main character, not an outside person. On a "Rhoda" show you wouldn't have a friend visiting who has just been divorced and solves her problem. You would switch it around. Rhoda sees something in the friend who's just divorced and, by helping her solve her problem, solves her own.

So you bring it back to the main character because that's who people identify with or care about?

I think so. That's not so important in sketches. You have to have the essence of what it is. But you have to know that you wouldn't do a complicated sketch on a variety show, you have to be able to translate it into reality—the reality of being able to be produced. No matter how funny it is, if it's unproducible, it's not going to be on that show. And some things come instinctively. You realize that you put the funniest part last, you build up to it, so that the audience is receptive to laughing. You learn to pace it. In the past I couldn't leave something alone for more than a minute without a laugh, but I'm learning to do it.

Do you test your material with someone, or are you a pretty accurate judge of what's funny?

I trust myself, basically. And I trust Kenny a lot when we work together. Each person has a censorship vote and that censorship doesn't mean of dirty words but of whether or not something is funny, whether it should be used. I trust myself a lot, though every once in a while I will read something to somebody to see if it's funny, or if I need a line. But I work from situations, not jokes. My main influence in comedy was Nichols and May. To this day I really do not look at Abbott and Costello or The Three Stooges, the broad comedy. When I heard Nichols and May for the first time, I thought they were funny, and it's not jokes, it's a situation, it's reality. You don't have to have somebody go out a window and do a pratfall for laughs—you can have somebody louse up their life in some way so that people watching say, "Oh, my God, I've been through that!" That's funny.

Do you have any advice for people who want to be comedy writers?

I think what you have to do is write speculatively, just write and send the material in. Everybody I know who got into comedy writing started to write for comedians, and there's no reason why you can't do that today. Comedians today are looking for material. I'm not saying it's easy, but they're always looking for the new person in town. There are two good positions to be in. One is to be successful and have them turn to you. The other is to be new and funny and have them want to see what you have. And it's a good era for women. I was in New York recently and went to lunch at Sardi's with eight women. They were all funny, most of them were comedy writers and using their sense of humor to make a living. Somebody said, "Do you know what would happen if this table were wiped out?" and somebody else said, "There would be eight other women right here, ready to take our places." And that's true, there are a lot of women now. When I first started, there weren't.

Was that difficult?

I always felt advantaged because I was something different. When Merv Griffin did a show on comedy writers they asked me to be on, and not only did they use me but I got the star's dressing room. I was always being taken care of better because I was a woman. When it became fashionable to have female writers I was offered a lot just because I was a woman. I went into the American Film Institute directing program because they started a program for women. It's harder for a man to get started because they have plenty of men, and woman are something new and different. This is a great time to grow up in comedy being female.

Andrea Martin

IF YOU ever watched "Second City TV" during its recently completed four-year run, you'll remember Andrea Martin as the portrayer of a stock of absurd characters in a series of innovative sketches. With Catherine O'Hara, she constitutes the female membership of the acclaimed seven-member Second City comedy team.

Andrea joined the Toronto branch of Second City following an impressive succession of roles in the theater. She appeared in Noel Coward's *Private Lives* with Maggie Smith and Brian Bedford, in *Godspell* with Gilda Radner, in *Candide* at the Stratford Shakespearean Festival in Ontario and in the U.S. touring company of *You're a Good Man, Charlie Brown*—her first job, captured just three weeks out of school.

When Andrea joined Second City, it meant leaving the security of a written script to improvise onstage every night, as well as appear in the weekly television show. It also meant joining the ranks of an institution, originated in Chicago in the 1950s, which nurtured such talents as Nichols and May, Stiller and Meara, Alan Arkin, Barbara Harris, Paul Sand, Valerie Harper and, more recently,

Eugenie Ross-Leming and "Saturday Night Live's" Gilda Radner, Dan Aykroyd, John Belushi and Bill Murray.

–K.B.

How did you become a member of Second City?

That just evolved. Right before, I was in *What's a Nice Country Like You Doing in a State Like This?*, which was a revue, with different sketches, and I was doing different characters. I think at that time Second City was looking for girls. It's always difficult for Second City to find women who are funny but still likable. Sometimes women are overbearingly feminist so they become threatening to men. They have a message so they become less funny and more political. And Second City's never been like that. The reason it's so funny is that people can actually sit back and be entertained at the same time they are getting a message. But they are never bombarded by satire. So at the time, they were looking for a woman and they approached me. I thought, "Well, I guess I'll do this." I was scared because there wasn't a script—just being up there on your own—and I'd always done scripted plays. But it seemed like the next natural step for me and I loved it. Improvising for me was always mixed with fear, but it was all my own expression. Myself. I didn't have to answer to anybody else and I couldn't put the blame on anybody else. It was just me.

Was it totally improvisations?

All improvisations, yeah. People in the audience toss out an idea, an event, a place, and then we do different characters that we choose and write the scene around.

But not just a scene—you write a *funny* scene.

Hopefully. I think it would be difficult for people trained only in acting to get up and create something funny. Maybe something interesting would come out of it, but I think you have to be a funny person to begin with. That's what works in Second City most of all. If you're naturally entertaining or funny or have an eccentric personality these qualities will come out when you're onstage. When you're really pressed, then you have to draw on yourself, so hopefully you're funny. As I said, some really good actors can't do Second City because they can only be funny through a role that has been written for them.

Do you draw on your own life experiences?

Yes, as well as on what's inherently funny in myself. I'm a little odd, I guess. When I'm under pressure, I must react differently from the way other people do, differently enough to be entertaining onstage. Most of my comedy is instinctive—it's not very cerebral.

Were you always "a little odd"?

I'm Armenian. I grew up in Portland, Maine, in a Waspy community, and to that extent I felt different. I felt that because I didn't have long blonde hair and didn't look good with a headband and little shorts and a tennis racket, at least I'd be the best in a class play. That seemed like the only door open that many people weren't heading for.

Where did the humor come in?

When I acted, it was always comedy. I never put on a Grecian outfit and recited *The Trojan Women.* I never recited Shakespeare. You know, I went to dance school and while everybody else was taking modern, jazz and ballet classes, the teachers put me in a special class by myself where I worked on little comedy skits, impersonating Shirley Temple, Sophie Tucker, Carol Burnett and others. I guess my teachers realized that here was a girl who obviously had talent, but they couldn't put her in a leotard. It didn't work. I don't know. Or maybe *I* felt that way, and because my feelings were so strong, the teachers knew I could never conform. Later, when I went to drama school, most people got off on Ibsen and

Chekhov—all the really great playwrights. But I wanted to do musicals and light entertainment. I think there's a place for them too.

You mentioned Carol Burnett—were there any other actresses you emulated?

Not really. I never watched television when I was a child. I sort of existed on my own. I had a much better time and more fun when I created my own television world. I don't think that there were any actors that I looked up to, who influenced me directly. I believe that everything I am today came from my background. I was funny for attention because I felt different from most kids. You know, I'm probably still doing some things today because in the back of my mind I want my parents to accept me more. I do it for my parents' love.

In Toronto, there seemed to be a wider acceptance of people with different backgrounds, and maybe that's why I stayed so long. I think most of the sitcoms today are made up of people who don't really have much technique or acting ability. They're funny because of their individual personalities, their own neuroses and they draw on that to be funny. Whereas in the days of Bob Hope, comedy was much more technical.

It consisted of one-liners, and not situations?

Right. It was much less subjective. But much of comedy today is subjective. Even for women—maybe especially for women.

Why especially for women? Do women have particular problems in comedy?

When somebody asks me what it's like to be a woman in comedy, my hair stands up. It's like being anybody in anything. I've never considered it unique. I just knew that I was funny and that I was a woman too, but it was never important for me to get out and express to the world that, first, I was a woman and that, second, I had something important or funny to say.

Are there any topics you really can't go into because you are a woman, though?

Not because of my sex, but because my concepts often differed from the majority of the other writer-performers at Second City, and the majority were men. So in those cases I wrote scenes on my own. I did a lot of one-woman skits on Second City TV because the men didn't think my original ideas were particularly funny, but I just knew in my gut they were. I said, "Okay, I'll just do it on my own." For instance, for a long time the idea of a Rhythm-Ace was funny to me. A Rhythm-Ace is a thing you hitch up to an organ and it keeps the beat, so you can play a samba beat or a waltz or rock or march beat. What I wanted to do was a scene around a Rhythm-Ace, but without the musical accompaniment. I do a character, Edith Prickly, who's rather brash and wears a leopard hat and leopard jacket. So I thought, maybe I could do something with Edith Prickly cooking with a Rhythm-Ace—you know, to put a little inspiration and spunk back in the kitchen for bored housewives. It doesn't sound funny when I describe it, but I just knew that it was. But the men didn't think it was particularly funny, so I worked on it alone and did it, stuffing the turkey to a bossanova beat. And it turned out to be really funny—bizarre, but funny.

Why didn't the men consider it funny?

I think it was an abstract idea that just didn't strike them as funny—nor do pieces on *war* usually strike me as funny, and yet I think there's a place for them. However, my comedy doesn't come from the written page. I've never been able to submit a scene and say, "Look at this, this can work." I have to get up and *do* it. I know instinctively it's funny. It's hard to translate that, to communicate that, to somebody else.

So you act it out and then as you're doing it. . . .

Then I write it, exactly.

Do you act it out in front of friends or by yourself?

I try out a lot of my characters and ideas in front of my boyfriend first, because being funny has so much to do with trust and confidence and relaxation. In the early stages of creating something, I have to have a supportive audience or I'm just not productive. And quite often fellow comedians and actors are too critical or too competitive to be supportive. I think it's the saddest thing in the world when I go to The Improv or The Comic Strip when the audience isn't responding and the comedians are struggling. It's really terrible. There's got to be support among people. So I try things out in front of my boyfriend or my sister or people I know will respond openly to new ideas.

Was there a competitive atmosphere at Second City?

Most of the time it was supportive.

Did you usually work together as a group, individually, or in teams?

Obviously some people prefer working with other people. There are some people with whom I never worked, although I really love their work. We just couldn't get a chemistry going. Mostly, I enjoyed working with Catherine. The pieces I liked the most are the ones I did with her. I didn't have to fight to get something across. I don't like to admit that, because I'm really not a feminist. I very rarely laugh at other women comedians. But there just seemed to be something between Catherine and me that clicked. I have an enormous respect for her. I don't know if it would be the same with another woman.

How did you two work out skits together?

She usually wrote the framework of the scene, and I would add the character and other little nuances. Usually the themes she wrote about were ones I could immediately latch on to. She wrote a scene called "Only for Women," an interview scene. I played the interviewer and she played a desperate woman who was newly divorced. I came across as a very strong feminist who flaunted her independence. "Who needs men? I don't need men," I said emphatically. "I love cooking for one, I love knowing where I am when I need me, I love waking up with the blankets on me in the morning. No marriages, no proposals, not even a cheap . . . one . . . night . . . stand. . . . Oh my God, I need a man!" I break down and both of us end up crying and consoling each other. It's how every woman basically feels. I don't think anybody really likes to be on her own all the time, although one puts up a good front. But none of the men thought it was funny: "Oh, it's all right, but it's not really that satiric or funny." But I knew it would reach a lot of women, and men too.

Do you tend to play one type of character—the strong, independent type?

No, I really do lots of different characters. You know an area that people can't laugh at? When women play lesbians—real strong butch characters. I've been working on a character—"You motherfucker" she says a lot—and I've done it in front of an audience, but unless I do it really broad, people are hesitant to laugh. It's strange because people laugh at gay men. There are tons of homosexual skits on "Saturday Night Live" and some on "Second City" and certainly on "Monty Python." But that may be because you actually see far more men than women who are overt about their homosexuality. Most women who are like my character, I think, stick to themselves, travel in small circles, and do not have a huge voice in society. And because people laugh at what they recognize, maybe there's only a small group of people who recognize these women. Before you can laugh at something you have to know what it is you're laughing at. I just did a screen test for an NBC sitcom and I had to interpret a woman construction worker. Now the producers wanted me to play the part with my breasts out—

innocent and wide-eyed. And *I* thought I would play it really tough, like "I'm workin' da construction line." They said I couldn't do it: "The network won't go for it, it's not funny, go for the opposite." I really pushed for it. As I said to them, "Look who you're dealing with, you're not dealing with Suzanne Somers, you're dealing with me. Let me develop something that comes from my own personality!" I wanted to take a chance with a different interpretation, even if it was extreme. But they wouldn't go for it—they were scared, I guess. Anyway, I don't play just one character. That's what's so great about Second City, being able to do so many different things.

Who are some of your other characters?

I play a psychiatrist, Dr. Sheryl Kinsey, who is a sexual therapist, but every time she talks about sex she gets a twitch. She's severe and serious and sexually repressed.

Where do you find your characters—by observing people?

Yes. And the character Edith Prickly is maybe a part of me. She's very loud, sort of aggressive, an "everything's-in-good-clean-fun" type. She just happened one day when I went onstage. Often my characters are inspired simply by a hat or a prop. I rely heavily on costumes and wigs and make-up, and that's what I find fun about acting. That's what it's been for me—fun and make-believe. I remember dressing up in my mother's bra and high heels when I was a little girl, creating a world of fantasy. For me, doing plays is like that. But creating original characters today is difficult because the minute you think of one you've got to go out and do it before somebody else does. The world has become so small because of television. Any idea that's remotely funny is prostituted, used over and over again, exploited. So you find you go back to what is universal. I guess that's what Charlie Chaplin and Buster Keaton and all the really great comedians did—they made funny the things that were most simple about life.

People have said what was wonderful about Nichols and May when they were at Second City in Chicago was that they used real life situations and human characteristics in their skits which are still funny today. They're timeless.

Right. I saw a French movie the other day about two elderly homosexual men: *La Cage aux Folles*. What's funny about it is their relationship. One of the men is a fifty-year-old drag queen and his lover owns the transvestite club that he stars in, but what's funny is how they relate—with others, with situations that come up every day. It's the way people relate that is funny, things you recognize in everyday life.

Is physical humor a way to heighten the comedy of a situation?

I think so. I love physical humor and do a lot of it. It's very natural for me, an extension of myself.

It's an area some women have found difficult to carry off successfully.

I think that anything that comes honestly from somebody, if it's funny, will make people laugh. Whenever I've thought, "Are people laughing at this? Will they laugh? Won't they?" I run into trouble. Look at Steve Martin. What if he said, "I don't know if it will work if I come out with slinky eyes—some people might think it's stupid, some might laugh." He just came out with slinky eyes and an arrow through his head and people laughed because he believed in what he did. He really thought it was funny.

What sort of things have you ever questioned doing?

Sometimes I censor myself on sexual references. I think that maybe I'm going too far. I did a piece as Dr. Sheryl Kinsey instructing women how to convincingly fake an orgasm. In a monotone voice Dr. Kinsey asks the women to repeat helpful "passionate" phrases like: "Don't stop, lover, please don't stop. Oh, you're good, you're so good. Make me a woman, big boy." When I performed it on-stage, I could hear the women wanting to applaud, but holding back, probably because they were with their husbands. Every woman identifies with that experience but not many can openly discuss with men the need to fake an orgasm. When I performed it for TV, it was cut out of the U.S. syndication.

I just saw the Richard Pryor movie, the one of him in concert. I've never liked Richard Pryor and now I know why I've never laughed at him on television. He must be restrained. TV censors what he does and he has to be careful about what he says. In the movie, he pulls out all the stops, he says "fuck" every other word. But it's honestly him and you are not taken aback by it. You don't think it's vulgar because it's so much a part of him. But television puts real limitations on you. Maybe I'll have to find another vehicle to be everything that I think I am or be able to say anything that I think is funny. Not that I have these great sexual insights that I want to share with the world, but sex is certainly a part of my comedy. Content can depend on your audience. Second City in Toronto attracts a dinner theater audience, not very many young people. They've really been raised on television— they don't go to the theater a lot—and when they go out for an evening they don't expect to be challenged by very much. I don't want to put the audience down because they're wonderfully supportive and responsive, but it's a different type than would go to a Richard Pryor concert where people want to see little truths about themselves uncovered. What I'm trying to say is that different audiences make different demands and in some ways you have to conform to those demands without compromising too much. But I really don't like to analyze my comedy.

You'd rather just go with what's spontaneous and instinctively fun to do?

Right. And I really admire people who have acting techniques that allow them to look and sound spontaneous even though they're delivering the same lines over and over again. I was in *Private Lives* with Maggie Smith and she delivered lines with the same inflections and repeated the same gestures night after night, yet she always looked spontaneous. That takes real hard work and discipline.

Do you, instead, try to bring something different to a role at each performance?

Not instead. But on some occasions I've needed an extra lift to get me through the performance. If I felt tired one evening, for instance, I'd try to work my fatigue into the character I was playing.

Was it a learning experience to see what would get a bigger laugh when you played the character different ways?

Oh, sure! It's amazing. What's really amazing is when you think you're doing exactly what you did the night before, but it doesn't get any laugh at all. It's sometimes perplexing.

Could it have been a difference in the audience?

I don't think you can blame the audience. The laughs aren't going to be there if all you're thinking about is how to get them.

Now that you're auditioning for roles again, are you finding any doors into comedy shut because you're a woman?

No, and I never have. I've never understood that and, knock on wood, I'll never have to. But I don't think I've consciously worn the label WOMAN on me, so maybe that's why I've never been greeted like that. I feel people accept you for what you think you are. If you have doubts about who you are, then people have doubts about who you are too. If I've ever had any doors closed on me, it's not because of my sex, it's because of the look that I have. I can't fit into certain roles. I know people who say if you're a good actress you can play any role. I've never shared that theory—the world is so big and there are so many people out there that producers and directors will cast somebody who is perfectly right for the part and no longer take chances on using one person to do a lot of different roles. It's frustrating, but I'm not bitter about it. I know that my time will come when I'll fit into something that's perfectly right, and until then I'll just put on different dresses and wigs.

Lee Marrs

IF STAND-UP comediennes are rare, female cartoonists are scarcer than hen's teeth. Thirty-four-year-old Lee Marrs is representative of a growing number of women making it in a small world—cartoons and comic books.

Humor is personal, but cartoons rely on an audience even more selective than that for books or film. The cartoonist is challenged with creating a world of impressions through esoteric images and limited narration, and if lucky, the cartoonist becomes popular, gains a following and gets a crack at the big time: syndication. The field of cartooning is not known for its high financial reward or professional recognition, even for its best-known artists. In the case of women cartoonists, the field is even more narrow.

Lee Marrs is a professional who has been drawing cartoons since she was old enough to hold a pen. Her fans include Ray Bradbury, Gloria Steinem and Herblock, Pulitzer Prize-winning political cartoonist for *The Washington Post*. Lee's semi-autobiographical comic book series, *Pudge, Girl Blimp*, is a masterpiece of character study and a legend among comic aficionados in six countries. Her drawings and dialogue combine to create universally familiar types brilliantly conceived and riotously funny.

Lee is a delightful, impish woman with firm, feminist philosophies. Her cartoons don't just lampoon the common absurdities of life; a current of compassion also runs through her work. It's right there on the faces of Pudge, Mei-Lin and her other characters.

–D.C.

How did you get started in cartoons?

I started drawing when I was two or three years old— just drawing all kinds of things and, because I read comic books at that time, I would copy the cartoons in the comic books. My family immediately drafted me to do up cards for people's birthdays, for relatives—"No supper until you get that card finished, kid." Slave labor. A lot of artists as children get zonked into that. But it was a great way to learn to draw cartoons, as well as Sesame Street-level labor negotiations.

Did you think you would grow up to draw your own comics?

I was a tomboy. I wanted to grow up to be a pirate until I discovered that the taxes on piracy were real heavy. So then I decided I wanted to be a cowboy but I discovered that you had to deal with horses. They were much too large, made a lot of noise and they could step on you, so I eventually decided to be a political cartoonist.

What do you mean by "political cartoonist"?

When I was in junior high school I started doing cartoons in the school newspaper. . . .

You did the drawings and the dialogue?

Yeah, I've always done that. I began in grammar school. Sometimes I would draw illustrated renditions of an assignment like: What did you do on your summer vacation? I would never just write what I did, I would also do up little drawings that would show what we did on the vacation. This made an instant hit with my teachers and then I could skip regular classes and work on my own projects. I learned pretty early on that things like the criticisms and sarcastic observations other students would make about the school would get them suspended or expelled. But if I did them as cartoons for the newspaper, then people would think it was wonderful. At the end of the year they'd give you a journalism award! So I thought, "Ah-ha! This sounds like a better plan!" I decided to become a political cartoonist and kept that ambition all the way through high school and college. That was what I was going to do when I grew up. However, I never grew up. . . .

How has your political stand changed since junior high school?

Very much. I was raised in Alabama where, if you were not for neighborhood lynchings, you were considered a Communist. My parents were super-liberal types in the context of Alabama. After I graduated from college one of the reasons I didn't go back to the South to work for newspapers was the contrast between their conservative slant and my liberal one. I started out being fairly middle-of-the-road and then became more radical as the Vietnam War and various other things went on. Like most of the people of my generation, I became more and more dissatisfied with the Establishment as my own experience with the Establishment expanded. I went to college in Washington, D.C., where I ended up freelancing for a lot of government agencies while I was in school.

Doing what?

Straight illustrations, cover art for magazines and slide shows. I didn't do cartoons for them, but I still did cartoons for the school newspaper and for anybody else. I'd do caricatures for the campaign posters of college candidates. Because I worked since I was in high school, by the time I graduated I had a pretty good portfolio. But I had realized that so many people went to art school and then for the rest of their lives they couldn't talk to anybody about anything except gesso, chiaroscuro or the relative merits of impasto technique. Due to my interest in political cartooning, I thought I would end up a double major in art and international relations. The best place in the country for that was American University in Washington, so I went there. Unfortunately, they kept raising the tuition, so I didn't technically end up with two degrees, but I actually took enough courses.

Did you support yourself while you were in school with these government jobs?

On a combination of my parents paying the tuition, several scholarships I had won and working.

When did you move to San Francisco?

In 1969.

Right at the height of the "revolution."

Right. When I graduated in '67 I worked sporadically in the art department of various advertising agencies, among other things, before moving out to San Francisco. When I graduated, Herblock, political cartoonist for *The Washington Post*, had become a fan of my work. He's been around forever, like Bill Mauldin. He had told the editor of the school paper back when I was a sophomore: "When this guy Lee Marrs graduates, you better have him come and see me. He really does good work!" Since I have an ambisexual name, people have always assumed I'm a boy because girls don't do the stuff I do.

What happened when he found out you were a woman?

He dropped his crowquill pen! After I graduated, I did make an appointment. I went in to see him and he said the classic, "But you're a girl!" and I said, "So what?" I had no idea of sexism in work. I thought all of that had gone out with hoop skirts. So Herblock was very helpful.

He did say that women didn't get hired on newspapers unless they worked on the women's pages, but if I could find a small newspaper that would take me on, say in the advertising department, then I could probably do cartoons for the paper whenever there was a local issue. He also said that it was a bad time for anybody—male or female—to try to get into the political cartoon racket because the five or six famous cartoonists were syndicated all over the country and so, for five dollars a week, you could get all the biggies. Therefore, why hire somebody locally to do just the local issues? Herblock's evaluation turned out to be accurate, but he liked my work and gave me introductions to several papers. They all reiterated the situation he had outlined. Since I was doing some freelance work, I could hold out for a while and not take the various government jobs, doing charts showing how much the fire squadron quotients had decreased in comparison to the bombing raids. I learned a lot in the several months I was running around looking for jobs. One was that many places would not hire a woman just because she was a woman.

Why? Do you think they felt threatened by your talent?

Of course, at that time people were not up-front about feeling threatened, and they were literally surprised at seeing a woman apply for a lot of these jobs. It was a new scene to these employers. A lot of the display houses I went to, places that supply department stores with the backdrops that go in store windows, felt that having a woman around would mess up the routine. There were all the tired old stories like, "Well, there's a lot of swearing that goes on around here; we're rough warehouse guys." In Washington everybody was paranoid about women getting raped and mugged (rightfully so), and they would say that sometimes there is night work and they couldn't assure your security. Of course, the guys got mugged too, and that didn't prevent companies from hiring *them*. But prejudices are rarely logical. But because my work was so good no one ever said that I wasn't hired because I wasn't good enough. But in many instances they'd say, "We'd be uncomfortable having a woman work here because there's never been one. There's just Marge, the secretary downstairs, and she never comes up here where we guys do this." This was particularly true of newspapers. All the old stories about the press room and the drinking were really true in 1969. I had a hard time even getting past the phone level with a lot of people once they realized that I was a woman, so I took to mailing Xeroxes of my work to people so I could at least get in to see them for an interview. The number of interviews increased astronomically. One of the jobs listed in the *Post* want ads was for a male graphic artist for a TV station. I sent in Xeroxes and got the interview. I went in and the guy said, "We can't hire a woman because you would have to work on the night shift and I'm sorry." So I began throwing parts of my portfolio in his face, saying that I could do all the stuff that's on TV. "See *this!* See *this!*" I literally browbeat the guy into giving me a couple of weeks' trial work, and within less than a year, I was the summertime art director. It was a lot of fun and I would have stayed in television if I had been able to because it was exciting, a new field. They didn't care if you were a woman as long as you could give them what they wanted.

Why weren't you able to stay in television?

The station had a corporate changeover and they hired an extra layer of people to be bosses *over* us! I ended up in a situation where I was in the back room again, doing lettering, not doing courtroom sketches or any of the good assignments I'd had before the new bosses came in. When I quit, and this was in 1968, just when the recession/depression that we supposedly didn't have started, there were no jobs. Period. Nothing. By that time enough people had seen my work on television that I had tons of freelance jobs and I didn't need to take a regular job for a while. But then my personal life fell apart and I flipped a coin to see whether I would go to New Orleans or San Francisco, and it came up San Francisco.

I really miss those TV days; one of the guys who was killed in Jonestown, Don Harris, was the director of the documentary unit in Washington. He and I did a lot together. In fact, we won a couple of Emmys together for some documentaries we did on the riots. All the guys in TV were just so glad to have somebody who had ideas and wanted to work. There was an initial discomfort in being "The Only Woman," but by the time I left we had an art staff of ten or eleven, and about half of them were women. That was really exciting and it was too bad that the recession coincided with the corporate changeover.

If you had to go back to a straight job to support yourself, how would that affect you personally?

After about six months I begin having chronic colds and I can't show up for work. That's why I've only been able to keep a straight job for about nine months. In order to not go crazy, I have to draw things that express a lot of my hidden feelings about what happens in the world; not just about things left over from childhood, but about what you run into at the bus stop every day. It really builds up a lot of rotten feelings and if I don't get a chance to work those out, I end up walking around in small circles yoyoing for five hours at a stretch, or calling up the phone company and screaming at them because they overcharged me 38¢ on my bill, or whatever. . . . Drawing is a kind of lightning rod for that anger. Instead of becoming an ax murderer, I became a woman humorist.

Why did you choose to focus on political humor?

Actually, the reason I'm not exclusively a political cartoonist now is that it takes a long time to discover what your most natural perspective on things is, and that is as true for humorists as it is for anybody else. The viewpoint of my cartoons is usually slice-of-life, not especially governmental, political party or international affairs-type box cartoons. In the sense that political issues are emphasized in my slices of life, I do do political cartoons. But on the surface they seem more broad-based than that. All my life I have seen things in a way that just comes out amusing—it's the way I naturally look at things. It's a matter of choosing which parts of that view to emphasize that makes a difference in the final product. It is true that if you have a chance to create in freedom, then the things you create come out of what is emotionally heaviest with you. A lot of times that is anger and bitterness, a reaction to what's negative. Sometimes it's because something really terrific has happened or you have seen something working well and you want to share the experience of something good working out. I think for most people, however, it does turn out to be that you become upset about something, really pissed about something, and then you do something about it by drawing it or doing a routine about it. The things that I started out doing in school were things that pissed me off: the cafeteria food being rotten; the fact that the football team got all the money and there was none for the history department; things like that. As my own world expanded, so did the subject matter—the military/industrial complex replaced the football team.

Humor has two essential parts to it: One, there's familiarity, that is, something isn't funny unless you *understand* what someone's talking about. So you have to deal on a common level that is communicative. The second thing is surprise. There has to be a twist or change that makes people look at what's familiar in a different way, or that points up something new. The more of a surprise it is, the funnier it is. This is the only sense in which I think there is a "women's humor." It's just like there is a lawyer's or doctor's or construction worker's or British humor. Different groups of people have different attitudes and experiences in common and so, if you do a joke that has that information as a basis, then probably the people who share that information are going to think it's funnier—*really* get it—in a way that other people might not. In one of my comic books there is an incident in which a young, inexperienced girl is dealing with a diaphragm for the first time. Anyone who has really played around with a diaphragm knows that the thing springs under the bed, sticks to the walls and so on. It can

blow your sex life having a diaphragm, right? But if somebody has never met a diaphragm, then that whole episode might seem sort of amusing, but it doesn't have that really grabbing, gut familiarity, that "Oh, yeah! That happened to me!"

Do you think that growing up in the South put its stamp on your sense of humor?

The South is still very much a storytelling place. People would never just come home and say, "I got hit by a truck today." Instead, they would come home with their arm in a cast and say, "Well, you won't believe this—I was turning into the shopping center at lunch time and. . . ." It became a story. That was the way everything happened, not only in my own family—everyone did that.

So you became a storyteller too.

Yes. I had three younger brothers and the only way they wouldn't burn the house down when I was babysitting was if I told them a story. They had to be good stories too, not repetitive: You had tigers yesterday—you can't repeat yourself. That Southern storytelling tradition was very strong. On the other hand, I was a very smart kid—tested several years older than I was chronologically—so I felt alien. In Alabama it was obvious that I had nothing in common with any of these people except maybe pimples. There was nothing happening. A lot of the humor was to keep people from burning me at the stake, or never speaking to me, or doing any of the other things I was afraid they would do, because in the South, you weren't supposed to be smart if you were a girl. So if you were making better grades than anyone else in school, you actively had to do things so that people would not treat you rottenly. None of this was terribly conscious. It wasn't like I sat down at the age of ten and drew a life chart: How can I survive? It's more like Pavlovian training of small mice: You try this, you try that; people like you, they call you back and invite you to parties if you act a certain way, and they don't if you act another way. You end up acting in the way that's going to get people to like you and accept you. For me, being funny did that.

At what point did you decide that being funny could be more useful to you than just _a basis for social acceptance?

In political cartooning you have to be amusing. If it's all dead bitterness and criticism, you don't go anyplace. So in the sense that political cartooning was humor, that's when I first thought consciously of doing it for a career. When I was in college I discovered that humor is a terrific weapon for social change. People will consider a new outlook or criticism much more easily if it's presented as a laugh. A most enjoyable way to *mold their minds*. My parents and my friends always assumed that I would use my talent in a career (although my mom figured I'd do it on the side while married and a mommy), and I've always been exceedingly ambitious, so there was never any question of whether I'd work for a living.

How did the *Pudge, Girl Blimp* series evolve?

I discovered early on that you couldn't make any money doing one story in a comic book. You really need to have a continuing character filling a whole book in order to break even on the money. But from having worked on the newspaper comic strips, I knew that if you created a character or situation that wasn't in keeping with your own life, you'd dry up after a couple of years and have to buy stories from other people. I originally thought I would do a comic strip about myself—I would do the story of a fat teenage intellectual girl being raised in Alabama and the various adventures she had growing up. But once I began writing the story, it developed into this other character, Pudge. She was totally Candide-like dumb, and instead of coming from Alabama, she came from Normal, Illinois, and was determined to go to San

Francisco to become enlightened—and to get laid cause she was also a virgin.

How did women's groups react to the *Pudge, Girl Blimp* series?

Unfortunately, what I discovered in doing women's comics was that the women's movement was not ready in 1973 (when the series started) to be laughed at or laughed *with,* even though a lot of us were very active in the movement. Again, the mass media seemed to say, "Well, this is just another example of how women don't have a sense of humor." That sort of bullshit. When the civil rights movement started, you couldn't get a black to joke about it. I was in the civil rights movement, and there was not a lot of laughing going on at the beginning. People were getting killed. Once things were more settled and people were a little less fanatical, then they began laughing at themselves and gaining a better perspective on the whole thing. The same thing has happened with the emergence of gay power. A few years ago, you couldn't do gay jokes with gay people because none of it was very funny. They were being jailed and losing their jobs—and they still are in some places, but it was even worse then— so they didn't think it was too funny. It does seem that for any group of people who are oppressed or trying to change their position in society, in the first onrush of anger and resistance, they need to stand up and say, "All this sucks. I'm going to work to have it changed." It kinda blocks out the sense of humor for a while. So although I was doing amusing, varied stories about women's conditions, I couldn't get women's bookstores to carry them at all. There seemed to be a kind of hard-line feminist stance, with all kinds of different requirements—like a checklist—and if every story in the comics didn't follow that formula they wouldn't sell the book at all. If I showed a man in a favorable light, if there weren't enough lesbian stories in it, then they wouldn't sell it. I actually got hate mail because I did the *Pudge* series, which had to do with a fat girl. The claim was that by showing somebody fat, I was ridiculing that person. Incredible. It just showed that the hate-mailers hadn't read any of the stories, they just looked at the pictures, had a set idea in their mind and condemned them out of hand. However, in general, over the years I have been surprised to see how many people really dig the character for all kinds of different reasons. The series was even used in a Boston mental health clinic as part of their therapy to get people to talk about their feelings of rejection. Professors have used it in college courses dealing with urban society. It's interesting because it's like having a child who is now well-known, famous, and having to deal with my connection to this entity who is not really me, but for whom I am responsible.

Tell me about the character Mei-Lin Luftwaffe. I get the idea from the cartoons that she's patterned after a real baby. Is she?

She is the daughter of a friend of mine. I went to visit this friend from Alabama who then lived in Hawaii. She had a six-month-old baby with big floppy ears and her name was Mei-Lin. Mei-Lin's favorite thing was to be held up in the air like she was an airplane, going "ARRARRARRARRARR. . . ." so I started calling her Mei-Lin Luftwaffe Aerial Infant. Her parents thought it was funny, even if at six months Mei-Lin didn't get the joke herself. One of the complaints that quite a few people had against women's comics was that we were not supplying the feminist world with superheroines—which was supposed to be our assignment. It was deemed that there should be a superheroine who flew around and rescued people. The fact that we were trying to work through all of our problems in our lives just like everybody else didn't seem to get through to people. We weren't *supposed* to be doing stories about our abortions in order to get rid of the psychic garbage left over. We were supposed to be thinking up better versions of Wonder Woman. The idea of having a superheroine who would fly in and change your life didn't sound appealing to me. It sounded like an oppressive idea. In reaction to that image, I turned Mei-Lin into a superheroine. It just so happens that she's only six months old. One of her superpowers is being able to change her diaper in midair with just a little ZIP! Mei-Lin goes around meaning well, trying to rescue people, but it doesn't work out too well. Eventually, in attempting to wipe out a worldwide conspiracy to enslave women by making them heroine addicts through the sniffing of women's magazines, Mei-Lin accidentally destroys the world. People are still left, but buildings, all of civilization, has to be rebuilt. That was interesting, putting together a new world in a few pages. So much for a know-it-all to solve everyone's problems. The point of freedom, I thought, was to solve them yourself.

When you had trouble getting your work published through the conventional channels did you consider creating your own outlet?

Yes! We ladies got together and formed the Wimmen's Comix Collective. We found an underground publisher who felt the women's movement had a market. Over the years we put nine or ten issues of Wimmen's Comix in anthology form. We tried to have the people on the book be beginners or newcomers. People would send us work from all over the country—from overseas too. For five or six years we had the only comic book around that was a showcase for new female cartoonists. Very supportive.

Where do you see yourself in five years?

Actually, I'd like to rule the world but I don't think I have the time and I'm really a little too sloppy and cluttered to manage that. I'm hoping to have *Pudge* become a book, a trade paperback, and some folks in New

York are working on trying to find a market for it. But you know, the most difficult aspect of doing humor professionally is selling it to your employer—not getting your audience to "get it," or even thinking up material, but convincing your buyer that it will be successful. I do both serious and funny work, art-wise and script-wise. Serious work has easily recognizable points of evaluation for any editor or buyer: clarity, plot, climax, believable characters, etc. Even for formula schlock adventure tales, an editor can see whether something works. But who knows what's funny? Humorists constantly run into buyers who say, "Well, I think it's funny, but our readers wouldn't understand it. . . ." or, "I don't get it, so no one else will." Humor doesn't often make any logical sense, and humorists are stuck with a search for buyers who have the same sense of humor they do—in addition to all the other restrictions of the market! From years of working in all kinds of publishing ventures, I've discovered that this uncertainty principle keeps the humor field from being as broad as other genres. Financially, companies fear taking a chance on humorous work because they can't accurately measure the probability of success. So, instead of there being any other magazines in America besides *Mad* and *The National Lampoon* devoted to humor, publishers play it safe by putting cartoons and humor features in dependable magazines devoted mainly to other fields.

What would be success to you?

Being able to pursue all kinds of different ideas without fear I would have to do them for free. One of the things I hope to do is make animated feature films. Doing animated films would fulfill just about everything I've been putzing around with over the years.

Do you see your work having an influence on the future of comics?

Fortunately, I've been around long enough to see it happen. European magazines devoted to the study of comics have said that the major direction of the new cartoonists has been along the lines we women pioneered: more reality-based, personal stories that reveal deeper aspects of life. We are credited with bringing new value to the cartoon art. Also, in Wimmen's Comix and other enterprises I've been a part of, I've literally trained other people, and folks have come to me saying, "I want to be somebody just like you." It's been gratifying and discouraging at the same time, because the whole field hasn't changed that much. It's a small, tough, no-money field. In a way it's like saying, "Oh, you want to be a kamikaze pilot? Step right in here!"